# Editorial

Back in 1996, Mark Doty reviewed *The Wild Iris* for *PN Review*:

> It is very seldom that a new book of poems enters the realm of books to be cherished, inexhaustible volumes which approach with authority the mystery at the core of our lives. Such books are perennials: they open as we reread them, yielding new meanings. *The Wild Iris* has the stamp of permanence, of lasting achievement. At a time when American poetry too often seems an economy of small gestures, in which limited autobiographical poems present the poet's life in restricted terms, *The Wild Iris* is a bold, significant book, one which quickens us, intensifies our sense of being alive, not because of any answers it provides but because it so resolutely embodies our mortal questions. Out of elemental but daunting materials – garden flowers, the desires and gestures of the gardener, the voices of divinity – Louise Glück has built as splendid, haunted and substantive an edifice as contemporary American poetry has yet produced.

A year later, Louise Glück contributed three essays to *PN Review*: 'American Narcissism', 'Story Tellers' and 'Fear of Happiness', and her books, not only those published by Carcanet, have been regularly reviewed, including Ulrike Draesner's German translation of *Averno* appraised by the Austrian poet Evelyn Schlag (2008); she also contributed an illuminating conversation (with Yvonne Green) to *PNR* 210. She talks there about *A Village Life*, contrasting its composition with that of her earlier books:

> The book was a lot of fun to write. In the sense of its being fabulously interesting and available. Most of my recent books have been written so rapidly that there's no sense when they're finished of any agency or role, they simply didn't exist and then they did exist and I can't figure out what I did. But *A Village Life* took about a year and a half which was ideal because I felt that I was always engaged. I could always go to the space where those poems seemed to come from and it was waiting for me. It was quite wonderful – as working, I suppose, on a novel might be –

She is clear about what she resists in the poetry of her more theory-driven contemporaries: 'there's also a contemporary poetry that's built on disjunction and seemingly arbitrary connections and I think those poets feel that content is sentimental I guess [...] Most of the work I see like that I think is pretty boring. It's very hard to tell one artist from another. If investment is in disjunction how many versions of disjunction are there? They're infinite but they have no character.' The poets of disjunction, if we can use her phrase, were those most troubled by her receiving the Nobel Prize. They provided list after list of poets they would have preferred, some of them conformant to the emerging norms that see artistic quality as relative and other priorities as absolute, and poets whose work is, most likely, generally unread outside the circles it traces around itself.

She is also clear about what she likes, noticing the work of George Oppen in particular. 'I like poems that swerve. They seem to be going in one direction and all of a sudden they're going in another direction. They contain a multitude of tones. That's what I try to do in my poems, get as many tones in the air as possible.' She is fascinated too by white spaces – between stanzas, at the ends of short lines. They have a sound, which may be silence or an intake of breath.

Colm Tóibín was introduced to Glück's work by Eavan Boland: 'I found her poems riveting and filled with feeling and I suppose that maybe that feeling is underneath – is an undercurrent – it's a very strong undercurrent and she can use very little means to achieve a great deal of effect.' We too were first drawn to Glück's poetry by Eavan Boland, and when I came to write *Lives of the Poets* (1998) my account of Boland was followed by an account of Glück, in a chapter entitled 'Language and the Body'. 'In an essay she writes, "One of the revelations of art is the discovery of a tone or perspective at once wholly unexpected and wholly true to a set of materials." This truth to materials – language, occasion, antecedent – is the proof of a poem. For the poet the question of truth (variously conceived) outweighs all others.' The truth is there for the *reader*: the poem in its full complexity and truth demands the readerly eye and ear. Sound is crucial, but active sound, sound deduced from the text and made by the reader. She has developed a dislike for a performed poem, especially if the poet performs: such reading confines and diminishes it, surrendering it to a shared occasion in time, to voice, and to the audience's collective illusion that any 'I' the poet speaks points back at the poet reading the poem as its subject. She resists the idea of inter-poem patter, of 'spoonfeeding' the listener, of directing the listener by entertaining anecdote and gesture. The engagement of a reader with the poem rather than of the audience with the poet matters. A poem is full of voices, and to reduce it to a single speaker constrains it.

At a time when performance is almost *de rigueur* in the poetry world, it is possible to see how radical the Nobel committee's choice is, almost, as it were, affirming the primacy of the art against the preferences, not to say prejudices, of the age.

The award of a Nobel Prize to a poet is a rare occurrence, to a female poet even rarer (only Gabriela Mistral and Wisława Szymborska precede Glück). We were thrilled and surprised when the news came through. At a time when other-than-artistic demands are made of artistic judgement, demands which have to do with a range of – call them – issues and not immediately with the art of the poem itself, it seemed a brave choice by a committee reconstituted in the wake of scandal, knowing that it would be subject to more minute scrutiny than ever as a result.

Glück's friend and colleague Claudia Rankine declared, 'She is a tremendous poet, a great mentor, and a wonderful friend. I couldn't be happier. We are in a bleak moment in this country, and as we poets continue to imagine our way forward, Louise has spent a lifetime showing us how to make language both mean something and hold everything.' – The poet herself is a little shy of the title. '*Poet* must be used cautiously,' she wrote; 'it names an aspiration, not an occupation. In other words: not a noun for a passport.'

# News and Notes

## Raul Zurita

The Chilean poet Raul Zurita has been awarded Latin America's greatest literary distinction, the Queen Sofia Ibero-American Poetry Prize for work in Spanish or Portuguese, sanctioned by Spain's National Heritage and the University of Salamanca. Raul Zurita, born in Santiago in 1950, has long been recognised as a major figure, author of *Canto a su amor desaparecido* (*Song to their disappeared love*) which engaged directly with the cruel politics of the Pinochet years, *Purgatorio* (*Purgatory*), *La Nueva Vida* (*New Life*), *El paraiso esta vacio* (*Heaven is empty*) and *Canto de los rios que se aman* (*Song of the loving rivers*). Chilean poetry has been rich in the last hundred years with Pablo Neruda, Vicente Huidobro, Nicanor Parra and – Zurita. He has previously been awarded the Chilean awards, the Pablo Neruda Prize (1988), the National Prize for Literature (2000); and also the Cuban Casa de las Americas Prize for Poetry (Jose Lezama Lima Prize, 2006). Previous poets to receive the Queen Sofia include Juan Gelman (Argentina), Nicanor Parra (Chile), Mario Benedetti (Uruguay) and Alvaro Mutis (Colombia).

## Everything Is Going to Be Alright

John McAuliffe writes: Derek Mahon, the doyen of Irish poets, has died at his home in Kinsale, Co. Cork.

Born in Belfast in 1941, Mahon attended Inst, before moving to Dublin, where he studied English and French at Trinity College, and hot-housed his own poetic development alongside contemporaries including Michael Longley and Eavan Boland. His first book, *Night Crossing* (1968), brought together poems written in Dublin and on his travels in Canada and the United States, and was unusually well received. It was his two 1970s collections *Lives* (1972) and *The Snow Party* (1975) which exhilarated readers and inspired generations of younger poets.

Glitteringly allusive, charming, formally commanding but willing to slough off big stanzas whenever the poems called for it, they epitomise the idea that poets could just go on their nerve. Their resonant, startling title poems felt as if they have always already existed, and others too, 'The Last of the Fire Kings', 'Afterlives', the poem 'Dog Days' which was lately renamed 'J.P. Donleavy's Dublin', 'A Disused Shed in Co Wexford' – each of them as lucid as they are ornately made. Long perspectives intrude without demolishing tonal clarity: these poems seemed to emerge from a Byzantium-like otherworld, seeing and knowing more than anyone else, alienated but with seemingly perfect recall, casting light and, just as coolly, throwing shade.

During the 1970s, Mahon had lived mostly in London, freelancing for various journals including *Vogue* and *The Listener*, adapting novels for TV and radio. Suffering from alcoholism, and the breakdown of his marriage, he published *The Hunt by Night* in 1982 and the first of his many books with The Gallery Press, *Courtyards in Delft*, whose title poem's switching of perspectives still astonishes: 'I must be lying low in a room there / A strange child with a taste for verse, / While my hard-nosed companions dream of war.'

Mahon worked at a number of universities during the 1980s and 1990s in the United Kingdom, Northern Ireland and the United States, but his writing stalled. Slowly he re-emerged, publishing two books which marked a turn towards a more relaxed, conversational style, *The Yellow Book* and *The Hudson Letter*, as well as plays (performed widely at venues including the National Theatre and the Gate) and essays, which collected old reviews, but new work too. His interest in translation, mostly from French, persisted, 'adaptations' of classic Baudelaire poems, classic versions of Philippe Jaccottet, and exploratory introductions to Francophone African poets, among many others.

Mahon moved back to Dublin and then in 2003 to Kinsale, a seaside town he had first visited as a student when he delivered an Afghan hound to Hedli MacNeice. Her famous restaurant The Spinnaker was part of the fishing town's rebirth as a busy, tourist-friendly resort. It became his refuge – he very rarely gave readings, disliking the circus of the literary festival and, after his early peregrinations, travelled less and less.

In Kinsale, he became fluent again: coastal sounds (*rock music* he called it, more than once), sealight and the endlessly changing cloudscapes, as well as a particular genius for biographical poems (Coleridge, Jean Rhys, Palinurus, Montaigne, terrific poems about his contemporaries, Heaney, Longley, Montague, Ciaran Carson) mark an acclaimed series of new books, two of which, *Harbour Lights* (2006) and *Life on Earth* (2009), won the Irish Times/Poetry Now Prize, while he revised earlier work for a number of *Collected*, *Selected*, *New Collected* and *New Selected Poems*. His work became a staple of Irish high school anthologies, and one in particular, 'Everything Is Going to Be Alright', went viral when it was broadcast on the national news as the Covid-19 pandemic locked down the country.

He is survived by his partner Sarah Iremonger and his three children, Rory, Katy and Maisie. His last book, *Washing Up*, published weeks after his death, will be reviewed in a future issue.

## 'The Muse really isn't all that nice'

Anne Stevenson, who was eighty-seven, and had been a contributor of poems and occasional essays to *PN Review* since 1985, died in September. Her devoted publisher Bloodaxe Books reported that she died 'at her home in Durham following a short illness.' She was brought up in New England but moved to England in the mid-1950s and stayed. Bloodaxe issued her *Poems 1955–2005* in 2005. She wrote a biography of Sylvia Plath and two studies of Elizabeth Bishop. She was wonderfully contrary in her opinions, based for the most part in her own tangential experience of the *soi disant* poetic 'centre'. Her character retained a specific New England inflection, which she evoked in a letter to *PNR* in 1998, quoted in Robyn Marsack's *Fifty fifty* (2019):

I have taken to heart your criticism of the first line of 'Arioso Dolente' so am sending you a revised version – thanks to you, better. Or I hope so, rhythmically surely so. The image of the jug and cup seems right to me; it was that image that set the poem going in the first place; it does accurately describe my mother's addiction to lecturing to her assembled family over supper every evening. She was an extraordinarily intelligent woman who should have been a history or English teacher; high-principled, well-read, a dedicated Democrat and ardent member of the League of Women Voters in Ann Arbor. The present stanza gives her more of her opinionated character (she predicted disaster for the U.S. if Ronald Reagan should ever become President. Clinton she would have thought a vulgar light-weight). My father, who was a lecturer in philosophy and a fine amateur pianist, always relied on mother to tell him how to vote. They were both first-generation intellectuals who met in their Cincinnati high school, married after college and came to England, where my father studied under I.A. Richards, G.E. Moore and Wittgenstein in 1930s Cambridge. All their lives they were determined to share with their three daughters all they themselves valued in the arts. I drank it all in greedily until I married; after which I rebelled against them and their Bourgeois Culture and all they stood for. Of course, now I share most of their attitudes and beliefs and much lament the amount of time I spent wasting my substance in riotous living.

Robyn Marsack (in *Fifty fifty*) recalls how in 2000, 'asked by Cynthia Haven about teaching creative writing, Stevenson said: "The Muse, I suppose, really isn't all that nice! She hates rules, hates conformity, favours her special pets, gleefully drives worshippers to drink or drugs, happily drives other worshippers to suicide, is politically completely unreliable, and, being an unmitigated snob, she takes flight as soon as she hears the word 'creativity'. Goodness, how she detests the word and makes fun of it over drinks with her cronies!"'

Bloodaxe recalls how, terrible for one who trained to be a professional musician, 'From the 1990s Anne Stevenson suffered from acute, progressive hearing loss. Her stoical response to this can be seen in her poems "On Going Deaf", "Arioso Dolente" and "Hearing with My Fingers" (all from *Poems 1955–2005*). A cochlear implant operation in the mid 2000s restored some of her hearing.' A few months ago 'she published what she herself called her "swansong collection", *Completing the Circle* with Bloodaxe Books. This was her sixteenth collection...'

## 'Poet of the Nepali soul'

Madhav Prasad Ghimire, described in a headline as the 'Poet of the Nepali soul', died in August at the age of 101. He was a prolific poet, and some of his poems are in effect national anthems, evoking the country, its landscapes and people. He was above all a nature poet in a nineteenth-century spirit. In his work an older, idealised Nepal survives. His obituarist seems closely attuned to the idealising aspects of his verse: 'He grew up grazing goats in the high pastures, roamed forests picking wild berries, the hum of the Marsyangdi River constantly flowing through his mind – sadly whispering in winter, gurgling with happiness in the spring thaw, wild and angry in the monsoon.' Can it have been idyllic, however? 'He ran away from home at age 12, stealing some money from the family coffers, so he could get a better education in Kathmandu – then known as "Nepal".' He studied hard and came back with a mission. 'Many of Ghimire's poems have been rendered into song by Nepal's famous musicians like Narayan Gopal and Ambar Gurung, and his plays have been performed for decades in Nepal's theatres. Generations of Nepali children have grown up memorising his 'Gaunchha geeta Nepali'. His critics suggested he was 'too close to the Panchayat rulers, helping Queen Aishwarya with her poetry (some say he even ghost wrote some of her poems), and supporting King Gyanendra's coup in 2005.' Latterly, 'some labeled him with retroactive correctness, as a proponent of a unitary Nepal'.

## A Penguin in a Box

The 2019/2020 winner of the Nottingham Trent University Carcanet/*PN Review* Prize, for the best writing student of the year, is Micah Gardner. The prize consists of £75 worth of books and a subscription to *PN Review*. And the University of Dundee winner is Thomasin Collins, who writes, 'I hardly know what to say. Everything is so up in the air now; my main plan is to keep writing and graduate! I am from the Highlands, but I can't be more specific than that because I moved so much growing up; my last year of school was in Nairn. I am part of the Dundee University Rucksack Club, which feeds my need for the outdoors and walking, something that was nurtured through living next to hills and beaches. I find myself turning to history in my reading and research, and my upbringing has made art a focal point in my life.' She shared with us 'A Penguin in a Box', an evocative narrative essay (*essai*?) that takes us into the worlds of research, heroic history and nature. It begins:

A penguin in a clear glass box. The quietly whirring air conditioning in the museum partially suggests the gales that whipped the icy plains, forcing the King Penguins to huddle in a family, protecting each other against the vast freeze. Now displaced into another kind of family, a visual display of species and specimens. The weak light above the penguin does little to dispel the shadows in the corners and underneath the penguin's cabinet. The fluorine light flickers and feet sound softly on the carpeted floor. The spectacle is worshipped and gawked at by students and scholars scanning for buzzwords in the clue card, a summary of the exhibit, for any link to the reality of our living lives. They only glance briefly at the figure stuffed into life.

*How can we rescue from oblivion these lives that were never made note of even when they were alive...?*
Shackleton.

A compelling adventure of historical imagination follows.

## Trans Issue

Much ink and rancour have been spilled in recent weeks over J.K. Rowling's original comments on trans-sexuality and their verbally violent aftermaths. The Society of Authors and English PEN have 'stated their positions on online harassment of authors' – a position which is so hedged about, so nuanced and subtilised, as to be effectively neutral. As a membership organisation, the Society of Authors is 'appalled at any kind of hate speech' but 'refrains from getting involved in individual cases of trolling, especially if an author hasn't asked for intervention'. They put out their statement in response to the novelist Amanda Craig's inquiry, should professional bodies do more to defend authors who are being vilified – targets for hate speech online, with death threats for expressing their views or, as in the case of Rowling, dissenting from the emphatic views of others. English PEN put out a statement against online harassment and supporting the right to hold and express strong views – so long as no one's human rights are infringed, a condition susceptible to very wide interpretation.

Craig, dropped as a judge by *Myslexia* for signing a letter defending J.K. Rowling, is 'horrified' that these author societies and the Royal Society of Literature had not intervened to stop the abuse of an author for her views of gender and biological sex. 'Coming down on one side or the other on the trans issue is very, very difficult and that will take a long time to thrash out. But what seems very clear to me is that they're not doing the other side of their remit, which is to protect authors. That's what really is bad. Authors are suffering and being intimidated.' *Myslexia*'s decision unsurprisingly provoked controversy on social media; the magazine issued a statement claiming to be supportive of any woman's right to free speech, but 'if a *Mslexia* judge expresses views that threaten to undermine *Mslexia*'s climate of welcome and inclusivity, we will always ask her to step down from that role'. Craig said, 'I was going to judge this prize as a favour to a magazine I've supported virtually since it began. I'm very sad, because I love finding new talent... But I am just very disappointed in them [*Mslexia*] because it seems quite clear to me what I am protesting against, like the other signatories, is the relentless bullying and death threats to a fellow author. It's clear that is what that letter was about. It wasn't about views on trans matters, which I know there is a broad spectrum of opinion about; it was to show someone I very much admire as a writer support. So it's disappointing and ironic that a magazine, founded to support and champion women writers, should have fallen in this ridiculous way. I'm afraid it's pretty damaging for them.'

# Reports

## Letter from Quarantine, and an Erasure Commentary

### VAHNI CAPILDEO

To cross the rightfully closed borders of Trinidad and Tobago, I needed a place in one of the tiny private jets that were becoming legendary. The weight allowance meant I could take one light-ish suitcase, leaving behind most books and clothing. It is uncertain whether or when I shall return. Apart from anything else, such as death, non-commercial flights are expensive. Pilots and crew rack up costs, doing their best to keep passengers happy, negotiate with the Ministry of National Security for departure exemptions, and deep-clean the aircraft.

A negative Covid-19 test within seventy-two hours of departure was required. While the drive-thru swab was taken in the driveway of a clinic converted from a private house, I looked at a gorgeous rose-pink hibiscus bush. A young, courteous nurse twizzled far up my nostril, like someone cleaning a dirty highball glass. From Trinidad's terminal to Barbados's transit area, I had my temperature checked five times by security and medical officials, and by machines. My cuticles bled from the number of compulsory supervised sanitisation stations.

There was no distancing on the transatlantic flight to the UK, and little evidence of sanitisation. Heathrow was the busiest and filthiest I have seen. What was the point of clearance to leave the Caribbean? Any exposure to the plague will have happened on landing in England. That is why I should be in quarantine, not because of my other country's status.

Quarantine, and thinking in isolation, made me dream up a strange form: erasure commentary. Erasure commentary would follow the course of a text that had vanished, unnamed. Tendrils of notes would remain, including distractions. The erasure commentary would deviate from what had gone missing. Its vine-like wilful-ness would be shown up by its own inability to refer to its ground. The inspiration for this form is partly Andre Bagoo's erasure poetry; partly an exercise in a workshop led by Rose Ferraby and Holly Corfield Carr at the Bodmin Moor Poetry Festival, where we placed stones on paper and worked about them in charcoal, without outlining or touching them.

Here is the erasure commentary on a vanished lecture on silence.

My author, who promised silence, is preoccupied with noise and power. Why? Perhaps the written-up lecture did not like losing its voice? Perhaps it guessed it would one day be erased? For each silence it circles, it draws tangents about noise and power.

This morning a church bell rang. It reverberated with my bone-cage. The reverberation was too much for the number of peals to be countable. I experienced myself internally as hard edges. My heart knew itself encaged, and soft, because it tried to ring with the bell and could only pulse. When metal bells water the air, I do not hear power, but time. Shaken by their expansion and fading, I know myself as a creature of time, a shape in an interval.

Such bells are qualitatively different from the noise of electronic ringtones. Smart devices pay us more than sufficient attention. Under their scrutiny, we feel insufficiently available, with our stupid habits of sleep and feeding. Scrutinising us, they are individually unavailable, like the powerful; yet they are things, answerable to other powers.

What is 'powerful'? Is it an extension of meaning, or a misuse of the word, to describe the image of wordless suffering as 'powerful'? 'Suffering' suggests the repeated passage of pain through a body. 'Agony' suggests struggle. I knock myself out in agony. I pass out from suffering. Without conflict – with no opponent but oneself, what power is exerted?

Consider the images of dehumanisation in *King Lear*, powerless to effect any transformation unless characters agree to be attentive to them. (My erased author is not discussing *King Lear*; I am.) Does Lear know feelingly that he is a poor, bare, forked animal, or is he making noise? Will the actor play Lear as absent or present to his transformative experience? Do we make the choice to be changed by the play? To notice its effects within ourselves?

Could my author's image of suffering be effective without being powerful?

The man tells me about a horror too great to lament, and I hear privilege. Reader, I am not his implied reader. I am distracted by a memory of shared horror, and silence. Political death was behind us, before us, and surrounding us. Then a woman turned to me: 'You have the language. Give us the language.' No matter what, some people will want words.

Why does the vanished lecture claim some horrors are beyond words? Is it a question of taste, not accuracy? If the author listened to the double-, triple-, multiple-entendre singing from Trinidad, would he be able to hear that however lovely and lyrical, within every song moves other songs, commemorating horrors beyond words?

Unworded is not the same as unuttered.

When the author lumps together lament and loudness, I wonder how he cries. Wracking sobs are not a figure of speech. I remember childhood wound care, and desperation. The attempt to make sounds surpassed itself in soundlessness. Each scream was emitted as a high, straining silence. Weeping does not happen from the eyes, but throughout the body. Maybe that is why he writes as if he must not ever have cried. Perhaps he has acquired distaste for his body. Perhaps he has cried a lot, and now he does scholarship.

This is an erasure commentary of a text with a noisy God: a God that speaks, noisily, and an author who praises articulation as if it were the same as volume, and volume as if it were the same as sound. I flit between books and find someone else's God speaking in silence, in speech that is the stirring of silence, a silence that – in more than one sense – stirs.

Decide you don't know someone because you feel you can't live up to them, though you are like each other. Accuse this person of hiding. Ask them to notice how often you stop talking to them, in between the times you bend their ear. Accuse them of hiding when you weren't looking for them.

A third person has no God. I read everything he writes about birds.

This erasure commentary occurs in a greater silence, rung in by this morning's bell. The silence did not become greater by reasserting itself in contrast with the noise of the bell that had stopped. The bell made the distance for the circle of silence it could touch. During the ringing, in the interzone where the after-peal met its own dying, I became aware of physical space just slightly bigger than my hearing could reach. Until then, the ticking clock in my quarantine room had set my horizon of silence. It belongs to someone else. It has a brushed steel dial with four concentric sets of rays, some of which are tipped with crystals.

Would my author have appreciated the silence of the hall where I studied for O-Level music? It was open on four sides – tropical architecture – to the rest of the school, which was not my school. Everyone studying extra music found a corner there. Studying music involved learning not to pay attention. A group of girls failing to play 'Twinkle, twinkle little star' in ensemble violin practice accompanied my analysis of scores and aural test practice. Their predictable noise generated a type of silence. My niche was where their playing must not, and therefore somehow did not, reach. It had neither power nor effect.

My author, why is your version of the ancient world so noisy? Is ancient architecture really so much designed to set apart crowds from the reserved places for actively silent priests? Or are you alone and silent in your study, whereas the priests activated their silence by co-creating it with the articulation, atmosphere, and expression of the crowds? I have known the most intense silences in the streets of Trinidad's Carnival when a clear moment forms, for example around two First Nations men, costumed as themselves, keeping their responsibility for the island's ways and intently hallowing the ground for the variegated dancers passing unnoticing.

The man is telling me of a fascination with silence, but not whether he means soundless or speechless, vibrational or still. He says 'silence'. What I hear is his sensitivity to 'noise'.

And you? Am I waiting for you in a tensed and sprung silence, or in a caved and open silence? Anyway, it's more like noise than polite understatement or rude taciturnity. Don't imagine this teeming awareness does you any special honour by having nothing to say. The words of my mouth are continuous with the meditation of my heart, and they are alike, not opposed, and they are not balanced; or they balance like the dancer on ten-foot stilts in Alice Yard in Trinidad, where I may not return. 'I would fall,' I told him. He said: 'I am always falling, and always adjusting. That is what it is, to dance.'

# Claude Vigée at 100

## ANTHONY RUDOLF

Claude Vigée achieves his hundredth birthday on January 3, 2021. He is the senior French poet, followed by Philippe Jaccottet (95) and Michel Deguy (90). He is also the senior Jewish poet, followed by Edward Field (96), Gerald Stern (95), Stanley Moss (95) and Nathaniel Tarn (92), all in the USA, and Natan Zach in Israel, who will be 90 in December. I have the privilege of being Claude's main translator and brought out two books at Menard Press as well as his previously unpublished translation of Eliot's *Four Quartets*. Along with Tarn and Zach, he is one of the few survivors of my own early and stumbling days as a poet and translator. I first met him in 1969, thanks to Yves Bonnefoy's address book. Claude was then living in Jerusalem, where from 1960 he served for many years as head of Comparative Literature at the Hebrew University, after chairing the department of European literature at Brandeis University for more than ten years.

Born Claude Strauss in Bischwiller, a large village near Strasbourg, he is the last living speaker of Judeo-Alsatian or Western Yiddish and the last survivor of the Jewish Resistance centred on Toulouse, which was independent of Gaullist and Communist resistance networks, for ideological and other reasons. "Vigée" was his nom de guerre: "Alive I am". Not being a foreign-born Jew, he could travel around freely after the racial laws were imposed in 1940, recruiting people and serving as a messenger between resistance movements. Eventually, inevitably, he was blacklisted and had to go into hiding. In 1943 he made his escape with his mother via Spain and Portugal to the USA, where he was reunited with his first cousin, Evelyne, whom he married in 1947.

Vigée is a rhapsodic and eloquent poet, with his roots in the Bible and Romanticism and influenced in tone by poets such as Saint-John Perse, Paul Claudel and Pierre Emmanuel. Claude is a deeply Jewish writer, not merely a writer who happens to be Jewish. Unlike Edmond Jabès (they were not each other's favourite writer), he does not revel in irony and paradox, he is not a meta-writer. However, like Jabès, he is a poet of exile and lamentation, exiled by language even in Israel. At the same time, like the prophet Zechariah, he is a "prisoner of hope". Like his friend Bonnefoy, he has a vast parallel prose oeuvre, in his case literary and Bible criticism, translation and autobiography. Unlike Bonnefoy, there is a greater integration of both sides of his work and indeed many of his books contain verse and prose, the verse generating the prose rather than the other way round.

His mind still sharp, his memory still in place, Claude, noble and stoical in adversity, is now blind and – attended by devoted carers – lies in his Paris apartment, waiting: waiting to rejoin his beloved wife and doctor son who died before him. I last saw him in February before lockdown. I phone him about twice a month and hope to visit him in November, if I get to a centenary conference in Paris at the Institut Elie Wiesel cultural centre in Paris. The writers Anne Mounic and Daniella Pinkstein are devoted workers on his behalf. His past and future are in good hands. As for the present, while waiting for the end, he surely wrestles with the angel at his own Peniel in rue des Marronniers, incarnating one of the three or four foundational myths of his ancestral religion. Claude will be blessed, there can be no doubt.

*September 2020*

### Post-Script

Claude Vigée died on October 2, 2020, three months short of his hundredth birthday. The centenary celebration will be a commemoration. In the words of the traditional blessing after someone dies, *Baruch Dayan Ha'emet*: Blessed be the Judge of Truth. After the news of his death, I phoned him in order to hear his voice one last time: "Ici Claude Vigée dans la messagerie: je reçois vos messages au fur et à mesure. Merci". "This is Claude Vigée's answerphone. I shall be picking up my messages as and when. Thank you." He was buried in the Jewish cemetery of Bischwiller on October 6, in the presence of family, the mayor and the rabbi, all masked. His tombstone will be raised after nine months, according to the custom of Alsatian Jews. This period is known as "the pregnancy of death", the length of time it takes for the soul to settle in its new abode.

# On Elly Miller

## GABRIEL JOSIPOVICI

Elly Miller, the last of the great emigré publishers, died on 8 August at the age of ninety-two, leaving behind, apart from a large family, three books she was readying for publication and a host of projects in the offing. The daughter of the legendary Viennese founder of the Phaidon Press, Béla Horovitz, she arrived in this country in 1938 at the age of ten, with not a word of English, but that proved to be no obstacle, and she soon fitted in with the high achievers of Oxford High School for Girls, where she was sent. The story goes that her father, always keen to find books that would be at once popular and learned, asked Ernst Gombrich, a family friend, to write a history of art for Phaidon. When Gombrich handed in the typescript he explained that he had written it to appeal to an intelligent teenager, whereupon Béla promptly turned it over to his sixteen-year-old daughter to read. 'I loved it,' she said as she handed the typescript back to him, a sentiment echoed by generations of art lovers ever since. From school she went to Somerville College to read PPE, where her contemporaries included Shirley Williams and Margaret Thatcher, as well as Ken Tynan, with whom she went out for a while. 'His friends thought me too bourgeois,' she told me, 'which I was. But he was great fun.' After a year of journalistic apprenticeship in New York she returned to join her father's firm.

When Béla died suddenly in 1955 she and her husband took on the running of the firm, eventually selling it off and founding their own press, Harvey Miller, specialising in science (he had been a physicist) and, her new passion, scholarly editions of medieval illuminated manuscripts, a radical step indeed, since the whole Viennese ethos of her father and his friends was predicated on the assumption that real art was classical art and its Renaissance revival. At her death, Lucy Sandler, the distinguished medievalist, and onetime pupil of Meyer Schapiro, said: 'No-one was more important than Elly in making medieval manuscript illumination central to art-historical study after centuries of neglect.' And, as if this and presiding over an ever-growing family of children and grandchildren, not to speak of cousins in New York, California, Israel, Belgium and Italy was not enough, she found the time to translate into delightful rhymed couplets the sharp and wicked verse of Wilhelm Busch, and to make up hilarious verses which she often sang to her own piano accompaniment at the birthdays of her children and grandchildren and of her composer brother Joseph Horovitz. An extraordinary combination of Vienna and Oxford, yet like no-one else I have ever met. She was special.

# Jane Taylor's Sweet Nothing

## JOHN CLEGG

Only the first stanza of Jane Taylor's poem 'The Star' is remembered, and then anonymously and under another title: 'Twinkle, twinkle, little star'. Oral tradition, as usual, has made a good selection, although the phrasing in the first lines of the second stanza is memorably strange:

When the blazing sun is gone,
When he nothing shines upon...

The idea that when the sun has gone down he is still shining, but shining on *nothing*, is irresistible while being impossible to visualise: a nothing made tangible, as at the end of Wallace Stevens' 'The Snowman', who, 'nothing himself, beholds / Nothing that is not there and the nothing that is'. As with Stevens, the lines make their own way through dense philosophical or theological terrain; they have the air of working it out as they go along. 'The Star' first appeared in *Rhymes for the Nursery* (1806), co-written with Jane Taylor's sister Ann, who would later praise her sister's 'inviting sweetness and naiveté'; as a poem, 'The Star', I suggest, is more interesting than that, neither so sweet nor so naive as a first reading might let on.

A lot of our attitude towards 'The Star' is conditioned by how we read the speaker: particularly, is the poem in the voice of a child? While orally-transmitted nursery rhymes in the voice of a child are unusual (the only example I can think of is 'I had a little nut-tree'), *Rhymes for the Nursery* contains several unambiguous specimens – all of them, however, by Ann Taylor rather than Jane. (And all of them cheerily atrocious. 'What a little thing am I! / Hardly higher than the table. / I can eat, and play, and cry, / But to work I am not able.')

What about internal evidence? Obviously, the poem's second line is the one pushing us toward the 'child' interpretation: 'How I wonder what you are.' Wondering seems a particularly child-like activity; the adult, we imagine, would *know*. But this supposes that there is a definitive answer to the question; the speaker would not, surely, be satisfied with an astronomical explanation. The whole habit of mind represented in the second line seems to me very unchildlike; a child knows what the twinkling thing in the sky is – it's a star. (Children are interested, obviously, in regressive explanations – but only, so far as I'm aware, in causal ones. They will ask long chains of 'why?' questions, but never long chains of 'what?' questions. This makes sense; language-learning couldn't get off the ground if we weren't prepared to accept words as satisfactory answers to what-questions.) The sort of wondering which takes place in 'The Star' seems to me to be characteristically adult.

The same thing goes for the blurring of scale which makes the star both 'little' and unimaginably 'high'; the separation of a sense-impression from its referent is something we only develop when we have a large introspective vocabulary. (We don't have to *learn* perspective.) The whole effect is closer to Pascal's 'silence eternel des ces espaces infinis' than any childhood naiveté.

These effects are potentially an attempt at a childish voice which fall short. The fourth line is different. 'Like a diamond in the sky' is a very unlikely metaphor for a child. The book was intended for children below reading age: as today, when its nursery audience came across 'diamond' I suspect it was for most the first time they had encountered the word or the object. Our normal reading practice with an opaque metaphor is to reverse the tenor and vehicle: 'The sun sank, like my hopes' tells us more about the hopes than the sun. What happens if we read these first lines of 'The Star' as being about the diamond?

It is tempting to read it through our own twenty-first century associations, and make the diamond straightforwardly an engagement ring – the Milky Way, perhaps, as its band. (Jane, unlike her older sister, never married nor had children, although she wrote several further collections of childrens' verse.) This was, indeed, one of the regular connotations of diamonds by 1806, although diamond engagement rings themselves were confined to the aristocracy (and not universal there: Queen Victoria's engagement ring was dominated by an enormous emerald). There had been a long accretion of diamond-sentiment: William Drummond of Hawthornden offers a seventeenth century example:

> This is that happy morn,
> That day, long wishéd day
> Of all my life so dark, [...]
> Which, purely white, deserves
> An everlasting diamond should it mark.
> ('Summons to Love')

Stars compared to diamonds is a cliché today; in 1859, George Gilfillan wrote in his introduction to Pope that 'There seems no comparison between a diamond and a star, and yet a Shakspeare or a Schiller could so describe the trembling of a diamond on the brow say of Belshazzar when the apparition of the writing on the wall disturbed his impious feast, that it would seem more ideal and more magnificent than a star "trembling on the hand of God"...'. It seems likely that purity, wealth, exoticism and engagement would have been the central association of diamonds in 1806, and that Taylor's metaphor would have still felt unusual. (I'm aware of just one previous example, from Richard Blackmore, 'Creation: A Philosophical Poem', 1712: 'The diamond is by mighty monarchs worn, / Fair as the star that ushers in the morn.')

Read this way round, the poem unlocks itself. The poet looks at a star, then sighs for something unobtainable which she compares to the star: something (luxury, security, a home and children of her own) figured in a diamond. This is unachievable, just as the star is distant. 'When the blazing sun is gone, / When he nothing shines upon': the sun, behind the poet, is illuminating a hideous blank, the star in front is inhumanly high. The final stanzas of 'The Star' detail the relations between the 'traveller in the dark' and the star – 'He could not see which way to go / If you did not twinkle so'. The star provides a marker for direction, but no useable light of its own.

There must be a grammatical or rhetorical term for what the first two words of the poem are up to, but I don't know it. It is not a straightforward imperative – 'Twinkle, twinkle' seems to me at the bottom of a continuum: at the top is Lear's rant in the storm, 'Blow, winds, and crack your cheeks! Rage! Blow!'; in the middle is Tennyson's 'Break, break, break'. In each case, a natural phenomenon is being called on to do what it would already without prompting. The effect in each case, I think, is one of hopelessness, and the emotional continuum is between anger and resignation. Invoking the unavoidable indicates, paradoxically, the powerlessness of invocation. (The tide did, one presumes, eventually turn for Canute; it must have been even more humiliating than the tide coming in.) As the violence dies down, the sadness intensifies. The destruction of the wind or the waves might be ultimately creative: to command the stars to twinkle is completely pointless.

Jane Taylor was not a good poet, but it seems daft to deny that the first stanzas of 'The Star' are good poetry. Familiarity with the words – not to mention the melody, an old French folk tune, a favourite of Mozart's, added sixty years later – makes it hard to properly judge them. In any case, the preface to *Rhymes from the Nursery* pre-emptively disavows everything one might say: 'In the *Nursery* [these poems] are designed to circulate, and within its sanctuary walls the writers claim shelter from the eye of criticism.' A disingenuous preface, which omits the right of the other inhabitants of that sanctuary to criticise: it is under their criticism that the 250 pages of *Rhymes from the Nursery* have whittled themselves down to a single quatrain, plus a refrain it never asked for.

# Letter from Wales

## SAM ADAMS

The hooters calling colliers to work are silent, the pit wheels that remain, confined to museums, no longer spin, the black dust has long since settled. But for something like one hundred and fifty years the south Wales coalfield was an industrial hub about which it is not an exaggeration to say a substantial part of British enterprise turned. You would think in that stretch of time an indigenous literature would have emerged to represent the place, its people and, overwhelmingly, the occupation of its menfolk. Yet the one title that readers, and film-goers, most readily call to mind as a summation of coal mining here is Richard Llewellyn's *How Green Was My Valley*. I would be the last to deny its power to hold an audience in either form, but it was written by an outsider who knew next to nothing of life and work in 'the Valleys' and, as I have previously explained (*PNR* 249), was assisted to his triumphant fictional debut by Joseph Griffiths of Gilfach Goch.

There are not many who, having worked for some years underground, found space in their lives to tell us about it. B.L. Coombes' autobiography *These Poor Hands* is a clear and ringingly authentic account of the miner's work, the conditions in which it was undertaken, and for what grudging, meagre returns, in a way that Richard Llewellyn's fiction could never be. The very thought of spending eight hours a day underground engaged in heavy manual labour, often in a cramped space, is enough to make one sweat, but what if you were aware of the instability of the rock above and around you? Here Coombes and his butties are approaching a section of the mine where there has been a fall. 'All alive it is,' one comments:

> Nearer to the coal-workings the sides and roof are not so solid ... Soon we begin to feel the heat coming to meet us, then we sense the movement of the newly disturbed ground; the continual creak of weakening timber; a snapping sound as the roof begins to crack above us; and when we are within a hundred yards of the coalface we hear the roar of falling coal and the sharp staccato cracks as the gas loosens more slips of the coal. Here is our working place for this shift. We hang our clothes on a projecting stone out of reach of the rats ...

There were poets of the coalfield, too, but they were few and, with a single exception, Idris Davies, are largely forgotten. 'Huw Menai' (Huw Owen Williams, 1886–1961) came from Caernarfon. He was Welsh-speaking, his parents near monoglot, and went shoeless, he said, to a 'ragged school', though that cannot be strictly true as 'ragged schools' were absorbed into the free elementary education system introduced by the 1870 Act. In any case, his schooling ended when he was twelve. At sixteen, he walked the length of Wales to find work in the Glamor-

gan valleys, early on (1905) at Aberfan, adding his share of slag from the Merthyr Vale colliery to the enormous tip that five years after his death cascaded down the hill to engulf a school and its children. What would he have made of that one wonders, for in his poetry a sensuous response to nature is ever in tension with an overwhelming awareness of incipient tragedy in the human condition. As a young man he was a political activist on the radical far left, writing essays in the *Socialist Review* and the *Social Democrat*, and making speeches on street corners, on at least one occasion, in August 1908, being fined five shillings for causing an obstruction. His prominent opposition to the political *status quo* irked colliery managers and he found himself unemployable until, oddly, he was taken up by D.A. Thomas, later Lord Rhondda, and given work as a weighman. In that capacity he was the employer's man, weighing drams, each bearing the individual mark of the collier who had filled it, and estimating the amount of slag or 'muck' to be deducted for the calculation of pay. The union's check-weighman, elected by the men, kept a careful eye on proceedings, but the weighman was unlikely to be popular. Huw Menai was again unemployed after 1926 and might have been expected to forget the favour he had been shown, but a decade later, in a letter to the *Western Mail*, 10 September 1936, he wrote of his 'very genuine' regard for Lord Rhondda, despite suffering 'insidious victimisation' as a consequence of being 'befriended' by a capitalist.

I have a remote connection with Huw Menai. I was told that when he first came to Gilfach Goch he was a lodger with my Aunty Sarah (my great-aunt, that is), before renting a house for himself and a growing family in a terrace a third of the way up the mountain overlooking two of the valley's three pits, named (I hope with intended irony) 'Fairview'. From there his output of letters to the *Western Mail* continued, from time to time varied with appeals for work: 'Huw Menai, the Welsh Poet, who has been out of work for seven months, and whose employment benefit has just been stopped, here makes his third appeal for a job before he is reduced to the necessity of applying for Poor-law relief for himself and family ...'. On 10 December 1927 the paper reported a court case in which his wife was accused of 'making a false statement to the local guardians for the purpose of obtaining relief', for the *Western Mail* had also been the vehicle of a subscription appeal by others which had raised £70-£80 for the poet. That much of this windfall had gone to pay arrears of rent is clear from another report in the paper, 6 March 1928, when the owner of the property obtained a possession order for a further accumulation of arrears. During the war he at last found work at the ordnance factory in Bridgend, but by 1949, when his cause was taken up by the Port Talbot Forum, Sally Roberts Jones tells us he was living on £2.17s a week. The

Forum's efforts gained him an annual Civil List pension of £200.

He published four volumes of poetry: *Through the Upcast Shaft* (1920), *Back in the Return* (1933), *The Passing of Guto* (1929) and *The Simple Vision* (1945): for 'upcast shaft' and 'the return' you need to consult mining terminology. All appeared from significant London publishers, Hodder & Stoughton, Heinemann, the Hogarth Press. If not lionised, he was at least recognised as a worthwhile and unusual talent, but that didn't save him from penury or near it for a good part of his life. In view of the brevity of his formal schooling, what is remarkable about his poetry and his writing generally is the range of reference it exhibits in literature, art, philosophy and what we might today call 'popular science', though that figured rarely in public discourse then. A teenage job as a packer at a bookseller's that for a time gave him access to an unusual range of reading material might be part of the story, but he was certainly a formidable autodidact. In the era of T.S. Eliot and Dylan Thomas (whom he declared '90% Bloomsbury') his poetic manner, style and diction remained stuck in etiolated Romanticism. Glyn Jones, one of the most benign and delightful figures in twentieth-century Welsh writing, yet with a keen eye for the features and foibles of others, is critical of his 'bogus lyricism' and 'debilitated' language. Having had a glimpse of the man in the round, I find them easier to bear, and when his subject is the pit you know experience speaks:

> Where shall the eyes a darkness find
> That is a menace to the mind
> Save in the coal mine, where one's lamp
> Is smothered oft by afterdamp?
> Down there is found the deepest gloom,
> Where night is rotting in her tomb.
> ...
> But when full work is on, the air
> Does a more homely garment wear,
> When sometimes, floating on the foul,
> Comes 'Jesu Lover of my Soul',
> Or, coming from more distant stalls,
> The rhythmic tap of mandril falls
> Upon the ear till one would swear
>
> The pulse of Earth was beating there.

# Concert at Walpole Old Chapel
## *From the Journals, 5 August 1990*
### R. F. LANGLEY

Fifty and more people in the afternoon in Walpole Chapel[1] for the Mladi Ensemble ... one row circling the front of the balcony – old men and women with their heads on their folded arms, chins tucked in, watching and listening intently like children ... white hair, black spectacles, sun-browned, polished bald head, one man by the far window (which the old lady cracked and thumped across to open, right back, then it blew to, so she returned with a book and jammed it open, from which something of cool air now shifts across up here) seated thrown back on his arm, unlike the rest, glum, frog-wide mouth, catching me looking when I do, the deus ex machina of the whole.

Young man, blue shirt, round to the north side, sulky Masaccio-type face, unmoved ... seated more intently forward, later in the programme, more obviously caught, by Beethoven's Duo no.3 in B flat major – where the dapper, dark-stubbled clarinettist and the more lugubrious, jokey-looking bassoonist whose keys click and clatter like machine guns in fast passages, return alone ... then in their last piece, the Nielsen Wind Quintet Opus 43, most intense and interesting, the main point of this afternoon's performance ... next to his girlfriend, with small face amidst abundant blonde locks, and her mother.

Down below in the box pews, sectioned off in units, boarded into little sheds in groups ... a middle-aged woman in glasses with a permanently smiling grin, sometimes tilting her head back to fix a sightless stare at the ceiling, a row of old men and women on a bench in the open, all tanned, white-haired, different attitudes, finger to cheek, head down etc. Old-young woman in green and grey slacks, with quietly carrotty hair the colour of the rawer wood in here, long face, ugly yet serious and original, with her mother who is on crutches, the metal sort with clasp for the upper arms ... she, the younger woman , being alone in a boxed set with her mother, puts her legs up on the seat, takes her shoes off, is flexing her toes and watching them , intensely, or fanning herself with a programme, or head on hand as a thinker, or just drooping, listening ... many fine poses across the picture pane, set against the wall.

The horn player, spectacled, bulgy-eyed, slender young man in neat pressed grey trousers and striped shirt, the very small girl flautist, in a violent royal blue suit, the jacket having out-standing quilted shoulders, the skirt tight, encasing her, conscious of it, twitching at its shoulder in the gaps of the performance, short dark hair, white teeth, red lips ... very very smart for the occasion ... the opposite of the bassoonist with his baggy white trousers and tousled hair and act of whimsy ... Christopher Card.

Ruth Watson on oboe – pastoral, flowery, flushed, whites of her eyes flash as she opens them wide, watching for the others to begin, lower lip set back under the protruding upper, round chin, rather shy, apologetic, pleased manner, big round earrings, piled-up dark hair ... all of them absolutely efficient, and by the Nielsen, moving.

The two big round-headed windows behind the pulpit ... opposite us ... smeared with housemartin shit from ... five nests as I count outside in the interval, over the crackling brown stubble of the yard grass. An apple tree with fruit out here, an old chair, straw, a garden, the white rumps of the birds going curving away.

From time to time all this goes away into the music, which is never overwhelming but powerfully blended, insistent and clever and bordering the tuneful powerfully ... the horn almost vibrating your skull, the others cutting fierce or sweet, adroit, twining, glancing, smiling, at each other.

Back seatson the balcony roped off with red cord,as dangerous? Stairs crack. Chocolate and cream paint, the shiny masts, pillars, the round 'buoy' with candle-holders round it which can be hoisted and lowered on a rope ... the pairs of oil lamps, white glass shades. The tester of the pulpit with bible laid on wide cushioned rest, lower deck all round, fenced in, wide enough to have chairs in there but here are none –the place is quite full but not packed. Enough.

The little oblong windows, like bedroom windows ... 5th August ... a Sunday afternoon, hot, but cooler in the reach of the coast's breezes ... the 'oldest Congregational forum' in the country, Charles 11, late C16 houses converted in 1689, compartmental, braced, pliable, snapping, maritime, sunny, narrow-benched, often shut, opened and known better now.

Driving deep into the field behind the next farm down, to park ... lumpy under the grass. Open fields, distant farmstead, trees, hot blue sky ... whiffs of sewage ... announcement in the interval that the sewerage has gone wrong and it will be healthier not to serve teas on the back lawn. 'They have had a lot of people staying', says a woman as we walk back at the end. 'The heat', he[2] explained himself ... white shirt, overhanging belly. 'We always begin with a minute's silence in our church.' And there is silence. Real silence, close behind the social and the music and even behind a passing car. Still there, reliably, covered not disintegrated, living silence. Birds' voices. Sussurating of leaves, tyres not just accepted in role but as thick rubber on asphalt, touching, making this contact along at this series of points.

*Edited by Barbara Langley, October 2020*

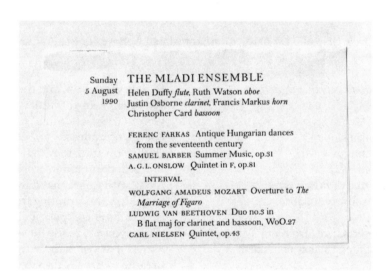

**Notes**

1  Walpole Old Chapel, near Halesworth, Suffolk. Now owned and looked after by the Historic Chapels Trust. They, actively supported by the local voluntary Friends of Walpole Old Chapel, are currently trying to raise £200,000 to replace badly-done plastering of all the exterior walls, which are now in a bad state. The Friends' project, Unwrapping Walpole Old Chapel, will let the public see the original underlying lath-and-plaster structure as the bad stuff is removed, 'unwrapped', and will share a wide range of audio and textual archive material about the Chapel's history. If anyone who has enjoyed this journal entry or may even know this fine building, would like to contribute to this urgent fund-raising project, the Friends would be very grateful for any contributions.

2  The late David Holmes, organiser (with his wife Linda) and presenter of the concert. From then on, and continuing to this day (except for this Plague Year, 2020), such high-quality chamber music concerts have been held, starting under their leadership, fortnightly during the summer, in nearby Cratfield church, first as Blyth Valley Music, later as Concerts at Cratfield.

# Poems and Features

## Broom, or The Flower of the Desert

### BEVERLEY BIE BRAHIC

*from* Giacomo Leopardi, *Canti*, translated by Beverley Bie Brahic

*And men loved darkness rather than light.*
John 3:19

Here, on the arid slope
Of that grim mountain
Vesuvius the Destroyer,
Which no other tree or flower cheers,
You scatter your solitary shrubs,
Fragrant broom,
Content with deserts. I've also seen
Your clumps brighten the bare outskirts
Of the city
That for a time held mortals in her hand,
And their grave and silent mien
Seems to keep the faith and recall
Her lost empire to all who pass.
Now in this soil I find you again,
Lover of sad places and the lost world,
Faithful companion of ruined fortunes.
These fields strewn
With barren ashes, covered
In lava hardened into stone
That echoes with the traveller's footsteps,
Where the snake makes its nest
And coils up in the sun, where the rabbit
Homes to its burrow,
Were farms bustling with life, and fields

Blonde with grain, and they echoed
With the lowing of cattle;
Were gardens and villas, pleasant country seats
For the pastimes
Of the powerful; they were famous cities
The proud mountain crushed
Along with their inhabitants
In the torrents erupting from its fiery mouth.
Now ruins encompass it all,
Where you sit, gentle flower,
And as if in sympathy with others' pain,
Breathe to the sky the sweetest of scents,
Consoling the desert. Let those
Who like to exalt our condition
With their praise visit these slopes
And see how nature who loves us
Cares for our kind. Here they may see
And justly appreciate
The power of their human spawn,
Which their harsh nurse in no time
And when they fear it least
With a slight shrug destroys
In part, and with a slightly more forceful
Gesture can also suddenly
Totally annihilate. On these shores
You see exemplified humankind's
*Magnificent and progressive destiny.*

# Benefytes and Consolacyons

## MIKE FREEMAN

*'What is it that has cast the into mournynge
and into wepynge? I trow that thou hast seyn
some newe thynge and uncouth.'*
—Chaucer's 'Boece'

Lock-down in Pavia prison, though for conspiracy rather than Covid-19, provided Boethius with reasons and time to write *De Consolatione Philosophiae.* Within the dialogue of his catch-all argument he inserts a sequence of poems, variedly metrical elaborations on his magisterial claims. In one of the translations that King Alfred commissioned those poems are naturalised into Old English alliterative verse, though in another manuscript they're rendered in prose, and when Chaucer came to write his own incomplete version in his *Boece,* he left the poems as heightened prose, albeit with his own parenthetic glosses. Boethius himself had offered a substratum of poetic consolations to buttress his argument.

Philosophy these days scarcely sets out to offer consolation, against Covid-19 or much else, still scrupulously unpacking our mind-sets, while religion, rather less scrupulously, is still justifying the unlikely ways of God to man. Literary critics as different as Arnold, Hulme and Richards suspected poetry could take over the space that religion occupied, poets as different as Yeats and Wallace Stevens offered secular alternatives, and Les Murray thought that poetry and religion might be read as luminous metaphors the one for the other. At least, though many a poem sets out to disturb our perspectives, the genre may tentatively stake some claim as a consolatory niche; the role of the poem at a funeral isn't as prayer, hymn or eulogy, but to occupy an accorded space of formally sonorous comfort. Even if written by kinfolk with more sincerity than skill, it is seen as a form of expression expected to say things differently, within its socially ascribed aura.

This isn't to mystify the matter, but a distinctiveness is discernible at two levels. The less important is a tradition of literary criticism that handles a poem as some sort of neo-Platonist entity, inviting an 'inwardness'

which must be worked for, worked through, as a secular ritual that teases out the poise of the 'the well-wrought urn' with an irreducible semantic as 'a poem should not mean but be'. Such sacerdotal gravity is an elevated variant of the pragmatic case: since a poem may well be multi-layered, so an attentive reading is reasonably expected. Here's the basis of the 'benefytes and consolacyons' [Wynkin de Worde]: an engrossing pleasure in the poem's 'materiality' that stretches diction and syntax playfully but pointedly, that deploys image and metaphor to raise intriguing interconnections, that shapes and stitches its textures and tensions by its formal structures, the contrivances you enter into.

It's a contrivance that requires your collusion with the author, a provisional contract. 'Kingfishers catch fire, dragonflies draw flame' – though they don't. 'Law makes long spokes of the short stakes of man' – but it doesn't. You enter there in the play of alliteration and image to be nudged into an imaginative slant on a sensory perception or teasing out an Empsonian quasi-logical trope. The reader's required collusion allowed a poem may be 'the true voice of feeling', but you're permitted to suspend your disbelief for its green shades, blue guitars, red wheelbarrows, and Les Murray's 'Absolutely Ordinary Rainbow'. On the coherence-and-correspondence theory of truth, we know the poem need not offer too much more than a singular coherence. Its *haecceitas* within its generic *quidditas* is no small consolation.

For Boethius locked up, or for us locked down, a poem at least offers a conditional completeness to offset the quotidian messiness, a shaped totality, even if it addresses disarray. During a corona pandemic there's some consolation in, say, Donne's 'Corona' sonnets, a ring-of-roses [yes, *that*] of poems which inject, inflect, infect each other; the poem as provisional contract where you don't have to believe what the poet believes for the purposes of his poem. In the teeth of the fatality statistics, enjoying his 'Canonisation', at least won't 'Adde one more to the plaguie Bill'.

# Wong May
## *translates Du Fu*

### Visiting a Nephew

To rinse rice
    Draw less
 Water
  Drawing much,
  You muddy the well,
Cutting down wild ferns for food,
  Don't let go your hand
  Let go your hand,

  You hurt the root.

### Not Seeing Li Bai

Not seeing  Li Bai
For a time
I begin to fear for him.

My friend
With talent enough to kill,

 : Be killed.
It's as well he was thought
Crazy.

Am I alone in loving that talent
Goddamn talent
One would wish on no man?

The speed with which he knocks out verses,
You will want the poet locked up & dealt with,

& his drinking manners,
      The insolence!
Drunk as a lord
Wherever he can make merry.

Friend,
Go to Guan Mountains
With your library

Come back
The day your grey head is
White.

### Dreaming of Li Bai

Parted by death, we choke,
Knock back the sobs.

Parted alive
Lifelong – we breathe
With regrets.

South of the river, miasma rules the swamps.
Not a word since your exile,
In dreams often
You made your visit
 Knowing how I miss you.
Your soul,
    Late of the living,
Blown in at first light
With the glint of green maples, out
Of the frontier gate 'ere the black night
Claims you.
They have netted you in the other world
The forces that be.
On parole,
Where did you get those wings & feathers?

Uncannily bright,
The moon too
Has no place to hide,
    Crashing through the roof-rafters
As it leaves the sky –
My absent friend
    I begin to dream in your colours.

The waves ahead are steep &
Perilous

We are handing ourselves
Over to dragons,
Friend

Mind the dragons
& other watery monsters.

## Thinking of Li Bai from
## One End of the Sky

A cool wind arises from one end of the sky.

My friend, I cannot vouch for your intent.
Migratory birds arrive & part
Do we hold them to their schedule?
How full of water are the lakes & rivers
In Autumn!

Good writing
Resents happy circumstances.
Good writers are rarely spared.
The demons of this world
Their gargoyle faces
Are made glad
Whenever men of talent hobble.

One ought to have a chat
With poets of the land
Purported to have
Drowned.
          The wronged souls
Whether freezing water is their element.

                    But for the likes of one
We won't see again,
Fish, fiends & friends

I throw this poem

Into the Miluo River.


## Resigned

Resigned from court!
Setting off each day
With Spring clothes
                    To the pawnshop,
Drink at the pier-head till drunk,
    – Who goes home sober?
Known for wine-debts everywhere
I have been around long enough;
 'Rare for a man to reach three score & ten'
Rare old times, chum,
When out of the deep seams of blossoms,
Butterflies,
Are seen
          With darning needles, &
In keeping with the surface of the water
Dragonflies swim, I mean
          Take wing

Go spread the word
We shall do our rounds
Here on earth with
          Pleasure
For pleasure,

The while
          Blameless.

# from *Bashō in Lockdown*

## ANDREW FITZSIMONS

A morning glory
    closing up in the daytime
        the lock on my gate
*asagao ya / hiru wa jō orosu / mon no kaki*

\*

To my brushwood door
    fallen tea leaves for my tea
        swept here by the storm

*shiba no to ni / cha o konoha kaku / arashi kana*

\*

In my hermitage
    a square of light on the floor
        the window-shaped moon

*waga yado wa / shikkakuna kage o / mado no tsuki*

\*

The east and the west
    the melancholy all one
        the autumnal wind

*higashi nishi / awaresa hitotsu / aki no kaze*

\*

For today at least
    let us all be the aged
        The first winter rains

*kyō bakari / hito mo toshi yore / hatsu shigure*

\*

The winter melons
    Each and every one with change
        written on the face
*tōgan ya / tagai ni kawaru / kao no nari*

\*

The year-end bazaar
    Couldn't I get up and go
        and buy some incense?

*toshi no ichi / senkō kai ni / idebaya na*

\*

I'm drinking sake
    incapable now of sleep
        at night-time the snow

*sake nomeba / itodo nerarene / yoru no yuki*

\*

Rise and shine rise and shine
    I want to make you my friend
        sleeping butterfly

*okiyo okiyo / waga tomo ni sen / nuru kochō*

\*

My father mother
    so very much I miss them
        A kiji calling

*chichi haha no / shikirini koishi / kiji no koe*

\*

My hair growing out
    a blue pallor to my face
        the long summer rains

*kami haete / yōgan aoshi / satsuki ame*

\*

In my tiny hut
    the mosquitos so tiny
        a tiny mercy

*waga yado wa / ka no chiisaki o / chisō kana*

\*

Day by livelong day
    barley in the field reddens
        and the skylark sings

*hito hi hito hi / mugi akaramite / naku hibari*

\*

A morning glory
    even one painted poorly
        blossoms with feeling

*asagao wa / heta no kaku sae / aware nari*

\*

Thin at the same time
somehow the chrysanthemum
in bud yet again

*yase nagara / wari naki kiku no / tsubomi kana*

\*

Out there in the world
it's time to harvest the rice
I'm in my thatched hut

*yo no naka wa / ine karu koro ka / kusa no io*

\*

A banked charcoal fire
On the wall the silhouette
of my companion

*uzumibi ya / kabe ni wa kyaku no / kagebōshi*

\*

Here on a roadway
where nobody else travels
The autumn evening

*kono michi ya / yuku hito nashi ni / aki no kure*

\*

They give off the look
of a hundred years the leaves
strewn about the lawn

*momotose no / keshiki o niwa no / ochiba kana*

# Has Chance a Choice?
## *On Novel Coronavirus, Poetry, and the* Pastmodern

### DAVID ROSENBERG

Perhaps we can now call evolution a poem. Most often it has been portrayed as a meta-narrative, the Tree of Life story. Darwin had left it open and latecomers until recently have attempted to close – that is, shape – the tree as it overgrows itself, visually unwieldy.

Poets, however, have thought for some time that evolution is more of a rhizome. In Christian Bok's review of Darren Wershler-Henry's *Nicholodeon* (London, Ont.: *Open Letter*, 1998) he describes that book as 'performing a radical autopsy upon the corpus of bpNichol, dissecting the ganglia of his influence, "the rhizome of an author-function in mourning"'. Nichol himself was reading Deleuze and Guattari, 'for whom the rhizome was a metaphor of the complexity of the world in general'.

Of course, this was not long after the death of authorship's heyday, if not the death of history's. We have since learned somewhat more: the rhizome of evolution carries human history along with the literary version. There is no building on Chaucer and the Bible, as if they were lower branches. And now we are reminded there is no leaving the viruses behind:

> Viruses are actually the most abundant biological entities on the planet. There are at least one and probably two orders of magnitude more virile particles on Earth than there are any kinds of cells. Further, at least half of our human DNA genomes consists of sequences derived from virus-like elements. Actually, the entire history of life is a history of virus-host interactions.
> (Eugene Koonin, designnews.com, 3/23/2020)

Suddenly, the viral world is more interesting than narrative trees. It is very much with us – many suffer, many die – yet it also gives rise to a transcendent thought: since viruses precede us, they did not need us as hosts. Not the human 'us', that is, but the supposed cellular origin of all life on earth. We archaic cells had to fight them off, at least the DNA versions of them, perhaps less warlike than a dance. The preceding RNA viruses may actually have goaded our proto-cells into existence, needing to be more safely encased in membranes – embodied, as it were.

It is surprising to find that Koonin's *The Logic of Chance: The Nature and Origin of Biological Evolution* (2011) has more to say to poets than vice versa. Chance is operative in all forms of poetry, but reading Koonin tells me that the larger chances of how the world works on the mind has long underlain modernism. A great reminder is Nathaniel Rudavsky-Brody's new translation, *The Idea of Perfection: The Poetry and Prose of Paul Valery* (2020), which includes selections from the notebooks on 'the construction of the mind'. Clearly, for Valery no less than Freud, so much depends upon W.C. Williams's 'red wheel barrow' chanced upon by 'the white chickens' – that is, chance may be gazed upon so intently that it approaches science.

We can see now, however, that postmodernism has ironized chance to the point we must chuckle as we read John Ashbery or bpNichol. Can hard science itself be funny? It takes a postmodern scientist to prove it, a great writer like biologist E.O. Wilson in *The Diversity of Life* (1992) or the evolutionary biologist Eugene Viktorovich Koonin, whose many papers and YouTube interviews reveal him to be an interesting English stylist (and a grandly Kafkan ironist).

Lately, Koonin's focus on viruses and the origin of life has applied to the family of Corona viruses. It is riveting to watch chance become intelligent at the origin or pre-origin of life on our planet (and probably other planets). Did chance have a choice? No more than New York School's James Schuyler's poem, *Hymn to Life* (1974) could choose to be cold sober.

Koonin may not have been reading such poets, though certainly there is Mayakovsky and Mandelstam in his background. In his *The Logic of Chance,* he tells us 'The title of this work alludes to four great books [including] Paul Auster's novel *The Music of Chance* (1991)'. Not many scientists can be expected to know of Auster, no less than poets evidence a reading of biologists (at least we know Dr. Williams had to read up on E. coli)

Has there been a more apposite definition of postmodern poetry than Koonin's 'this crucial relationship between chance and necessity. I make the case that variously constrained randomness is at the very heart of the entire history of life'?

Frank O'Hara, who made much of 'process' in his essays on art (but who was ticked off by his contemporary Charles Olson's philosophizing on it) might have unwound and been delighted by Koonin's more recent assertion of our 'transition to a postmodern view of life. Essentially, this signifies the plurality of pattern and process in evolution; the central role of contingency in the evolution of life forms ('evolution as tinkering')'. O'Hara may have deemed Jackson Pollock a major tinkerer, but only now, were he alive, would Frank (I never heard anyone refer to him as 'O'Hara') be satisfied to know his views applied to *all* life forms.

If Koonin had read Frank's major poem 'Second Avenue' (1960) he would have called the rise of prokaryotes on earth 'an action poem':

> This is a large poem to maintain without a narrator; but, on the other hand, the situation removes the ego of the poem [or poet] from the process of the poem and then allows a multitude of gestures to run in at all points. It could be called an 'action poem'. Like

Pollock, who created a procedure of it.
(Butterick and Bertholf, Poetry Foundation)

On the other hand, I would wrap the viral world today into more than an action painting and call it 'species consciousness'. There are more species of viruses than fauna and flora on our planet. If we are conscious of this fact, we become more aware of our human dependence on natural processes, namely replication errors in evolution that are inherited and allow for new species like our own. We can thank heaven, both for errors and their evolutionary otherness, though they are rare. Other people seem to us quite common, which may be why it's harder to appreciate them in their individual otherness.

However, we must now understand we are each a cosmos of species, our bodies made up of hundreds of interacting species of microbes. While our ability to interpret the invisible is perhaps unique among mammals, we have miles to go before internalizing this awareness. Meanwhile, the mass of humanity still tends to believe what they see or hear. Most of us are aware of the interplay between fictional representations of verisimilitude and the selling of a product in advertisements, yet many are today challenged by competing narratives (political, scientific, etc.) in the reportage of the novel Corona pandemic. News and entertainment grow indistinguishable in their narratives without a *contextual* awareness of narratives, which can resemble advertisements for ending the pandemic with a wish. Wishes, or thoughts, are something the late poet Kenneth Koch – building upon Freud's 1900 dream book – characterized in his poetry textbook, *Wishes, Lies, and Dreams* (1970). That is, not to simply wish a thing gone but to vaccinate the wish in a poem that, in Emersonian terms, allows us to become cosmically aware of the thinking self.

Similarly, as most evolutionary scientists wish, along with Koonin and many of us, we hope to eventually find 'how chemical systems on the early Earth might have provided the precursor molecules necessary for self-replication'. As even archaic poets knew, however, 'self-replication' has always been our human poetry, no matter how totemic. Supernatural representations of us replicating into (or from) an afterlife are hardly different, yet modernism can seem to relegate them to wishes, lies, and dreams – or more longingly, 'presences', as emphasized in a new translation of Yves Bonnefoy's essays.

I have quoted Koonin's description of the Tree of Life (the evolutionary model) as a meta-narrative, a consciousness of narrative. Was this as true of Eden represented by the Hebraic poet in Genesis? Of course. No one was taking dictation from Satan wrapped snakishly around the Tree of Knowledge; we accept it as a meta-narrative, as a poem.

However many interpretive mutations come down to us, the Garden of Eden is immutable as a Genesis text. While Covid-19 (the disease) is likely to mutate, and we are still needing to interpret not only the latest one but many more in the Corona family (for instance those that cause common colds) Corona is immutable, inhabiting far more animal species than our own. If we can accept Corona as part of our selves (as if within the poem of our selfhood) it enlarges our knowledge of natural selection,

by which our human species was naturally created.

Nevertheless, 'natural selection has no analogy with any aspect of human behavior', wrote the late François Jacob ('Evolution and Tinkering', *Science*, 1977), who exerted a strong influence on Koonin. 'However, if one wants to play with a comparison,' writes Koonin, 'one would have to say that natural selection does not work like an engineer works. It works like a tinkerer – a tinkerer who does not know exactly what he is going to produce but uses whatever he finds around him whether it be pieces of string, fragments of wood, or old cardboards; in short, it works like a tinkerer who uses everything at his disposal to produce some kind of workable object.' (*The Logic of Life*, 1991).

This sounds like a poet, doesn't it? Not simply the poet defined by a book on prosody, but a kind of blind watchmaker with infinite time on her hands. Homo sapiens have always lived within the confined time and space of civilization as self-domesticated animals. So, if our culture, now under stress by the novel Covid-19, can learn to study ecosystems (in which microbe species far outnumber visible ones) 'a new anthropological transition will take us out of the Neolithic mentality toward a new type of psyche'. (*How We Became Sapiens*, Silvana Condemi and Francois Savatier, 2019).

Condemi and Savatier suggest their 'new type' of psyche will be digitally wired, yet they were writing just before the pandemic. We might say now that it will be determined by virtual tech, allowing us to let more land become 're-wilded', as these anthropologists wish. First, however, we'll need our psyches also to be re-wilded, in the sense of re-studying our ecosystem origins, merging natural history with, for instance, the ancient literary history of the Garden of Eden.

Hebraic poets wrote that Garden epic – what do we know of them? Further, what do we know of the origin of poetry? My guess is that it began in the trees. Think of Howler monkeys, for whom vocal communication forms an important part of their social behavior. Further, they can smell out food (primarily fruit) up to two kilometres away. John Lloyd Stephens described the howler monkeys at the Maya ruins of Copan as 'grave and solemn, almost emotionally wounded, as if officiating as the guardians of consecrated ground'. To the Mayas of the Classic period, 'they were the divine patrons of the artisans, especially scribes'. Maya or Hebraic, molecular or evolutionary biologist, the poetry of sound and genes conveyed a history of origins.

Even when our computers and AI become breathtaking watchmakers with their processes ever more invisible, the countless invisible species of an ecosystem precede us, including the first forms of life, viruses, 'which allowed us to become who we are', as Alexander Van Tulleken phrases it in a recent *TLS* review (8/21/20) of books on the current pandemic. Will we need a new psyche to hold equally in mind disease and creation, or could a future poet's Darwinian translation of Genesis suffice – a poet whom I would suggest might best be called *pastmodern*?

Having spoken of the evolutionary tree of life should also suggest the original Tree of Life, among the two unique trees at the center of the Garden of Eden. Likewise metaphorical, it's not until now that the tree beside it, the Tree of Knowledge, has helped us to uncover a theory of the origin of life. To scientists, their version may seem to be more compelling, even moving, than the supernatural version. However, it lacks for now the luster of the miraculous, something that suggests to a poet like the late Yves Bonnefoy, 'the truth of the instant in opposition to the timelessness of scientific formulas or the experimentations of play' (trans. Rudolf, in *Yves Bonnefoy: Prose,* 2020).

Such an instant, Bonnefoy might say, is Eve's bite into the apple, a specific moment in time (he equates it with a 'gaze', such as the serpent's upon Eve) that makes it historical on the scale of myth, transcendent. It was *necessary* to who we are, Koonin would say, that Eve *chanced* upon Lucifer by the tree, an irrevocable moment of 'presence' in Bonnefoy's terms, though in Koonin's terms, 'I make the case that *variously constrained randomness* is at the very heart of the entire history of life'.

It is rather uncanny for Genesis and trees that, *pace* Koonin, 'although no single tree can fully represent the evolution of complete genomes and the respective life forms...these components can be revealed through the analysis of the Forest of Life (FOL), the complete collection of phylogenetic trees for individual genes'. Perhaps even the FOL might be contained within Eden's Tree of Knowledge, while genomics could be represented in a cosmic poem as a combination of content or words (genes) and form (genome). Still, Eve was already breathing, as was the serpent in order to speak to her, so that *he,* Lucifer, inhabits the place of an author, a small-c creator.

For the time being, the question of whether Lucifer or other angels breathed oxygen in heaven is moot; likewise, the old idea that viruses were only 'non-breathing' parasites is now roughly equivalent to saying that poems are parasitic forms that rely upon content for life. According to Koonin, the opposite is true: without form, there would not only be no poetry, there would be no content. It suggests that poetry gives life to the verbal language that characterizes our species.

We could say the poetry of evolution interprets the world similarly, by the incessant chances of words or genes folded into a formal membrane enclosing the content of a discrete form of life. That is, a membrane of music enlivens a cell filled with protein content. But the music can't start until viral forms ('outside' genetic material) play upon it.

The virus upon which Eugene Koonin gazes in a 21st century computer, however, is a presence at the origin of life. Whether it was a supernatural origin, as in Genesis, or a creature of chance, its creation was necessary – as much so as is ours, verified in our gaze upon life as necessarily being there. When we see the virus magnified it unfolds less of its presence than the mathematical gaze of computational biology, where its presence unscrolls from its RNA origin. Or further back: 'the principal lineages of viruses and related selfish agents emerged from the primordial pool of primitive genetic elements, the ancestors of both cellular and viral genes,' in Koonin's words. Although he copped the word 'selfish'

from Richard Dawkins's *The Selfish Gene*, Koonin is more ironic. His ancestral 'genetic elements' of life, being less selfish, are even greater presences. All the more so because they can't be seen, but only gazed upon as if supernatural. Let's take it a step further and call that 'primordial pool' poetry, as Gertrude Stein would, so that we become poetic creatures, created out of it like poems chanced with no narrative beginning or end – or at least, not necessarily so.

For Koonin, it's a cosmic poem, just as chance is absolutely necessary for natural selection, the driver of evolution. In ancient myths and religion, the gods or God is the driver of creation, a necessity equal to chance. Like chance, the gods are beyond unpredictable, they represent the unknowable. So we have to acknowledge a supernatural unknowability behind chance that resembles the cosmic poetry of ancient texts.

'All presence of the self is, moreover, a unity,' writes Bonnefoy on Giacometti, 'transcending the material aspect of eyes, nose or mouth, to release a face. But these components are also something material, an outside where nothingness loiters, and likeness is therefore a trap: we must look for its invisible background, we must destroy likeness as well as question it....It is here that Giacometti is modern – because the myths that used to sustain the experience of presence have collapsed.' In place of the pre-modern myth of likeness, we have the chance results of questioning, just as the art of photography questions likeness for the invisible instant of time – or what Bonnefoy calls 'presence'.

Neither Freud nor Bonnefoy had yet encountered the quantum indeterminacy of evolutionary biology. Koonin describes it as postmodernist:

Whatever one thinks of the postmodern philosophy, its worldview certainly emphasizes the richness and extreme diversity of the processes and patterns that constitute reality. Such is the complexity of these multiple trends that, to some philosophers of the post-modern ilk, any major generalization is anathema. In today's evolutionary biology, the plurality of processes and patterns is arguably the main theme; if we want to speak in paradoxes, it could be said that 'the main theme is the absence of an overarching main theme.

Instead of poetry preceding science, we may now hope that a silver lining to Koonin's *The Logic of Chance* is stimulated by the novel Corona, so that poetry may loosen up its resistance to cosmic creation (big C or little c), as in no less than Milton: 'Was I deceiv'd, or did a sable cloud/ Turn forth her silver lining on the night?' (*Comus,* 1634). The question of deception for Milton here was one of creating a masque as anti-masque, very anti-matter-ish. And very natural of him to soon engage the Garden of Eden on a cosmic scale. While *Paradise Lost* has a basically moral dimension in its depiction of human creation, in tune with the Hebrew, the intervention of Satan leaves us forever open to chance in the war of good and evil. I'd say the same for the war between virus and antibody, though certainly we must survive in order to praise our humanity. Does Nature, no less than God, have a say in this? Perhaps only a poet can say today, if he/she follows Koonin back to life's creation in prehistory.

As much as science and literature need each other, it's appalling how little these disciplines engage. Much blame seems to lie in the increasing proliferation and subsequent isolation of academic departments. 'Interdisciplinary' and 'comparative', the old buzzwords, have become conventionally dull. Comparing apples and oranges is something, but in the end you are still in the fruit business. Who is comparing apples and Lagrange points, capsids and prose poems? Here is Koonin on the protein capsid that surrounds a virus and reminds us of an organic cell's necessary membrane:

> Viruses with the largest genomes encode a panoply of diverse proteins involved in repair processes, membrane trafficking, a variety of metabolic pathways, and, in some cases, even translation system components.

Apart from sounding like a text in linguistics, consider the metaphorical 'membrane trafficking': the virus as drug dealer, or what is called 'the man' in junkie parlance. And then, in explaining one of several theories, 'viruses were once part of the genetic material of host cells but escaped cell control and later evolved by pickpocketing genes via horizontal gene transfer (HGT)'. The little criminals! Incidentally, HGT is genomic-speak for rhizome. And further texture: 'a fully fledged membrane'; 'translation machineries'; 'motors for DNA or RNA packaging'; 'omnis virus e virus, a play on omnis cellula e cellula.'

These instances of metaphoric appropriation suggest as well the embedding of human evolution in a much deeper history – events awaiting their *pastmodern* poems, along with those events in our cultural evolution: imagining the poets behind the Homeric and Sumerian Odes, for instance, or lyrical urges of the poets in the Bible's Book of Proverbs. Some embryonic *pastmodern* contemporary poets I would cite, in the sense of their experimental translation projects, include Alice Oswald, A.E. Stallings, Anne Carson, Gabriel Levin, and Sarah Ruden, as well as instances of the Gilgamesh epic's appropriation that Michael Schmidt turns up in his *Gilgamesh: The Life of a Poem* (2019). An early *pastmodern* work still flying below the canonical radar, bpNichol's lifelong poem, *The Martyrology* (Toronto, 1969) proposes its own cosmology of saints and supernovae while reaching back to Biblical and Akkadian texts, and creating as well a mythopoetics that ranges through Freud, Wittgenstein, Apollinaire and Philip Whalen, to name a few. Frank Davey's lifelong engagement with that poem and its late poet, *Everybody's Martyrology,* has just appeared (Toronto, 2020).

Were Harold Bloom still alive to note that all the death and despair in *The Waste Land* incorporates the aftermath of the 1917 flu pandemic, his contemporary students might shake their internal heads, more likely assuming it a misreading (or missed reading) on both Eliot and Bloom's part of *Das Kapital*. On a more personal note, it was the contemporary poet Grace Schulman, still teaching poetry at CUNY, who pointed out the 1917 flu influence to me, alert to it via her late husband, a pioneering virologist. I've also had the luck to be married to a research scientist long working in HIV studies and now immersed in novel Corona parallels (or lack of them). It was she who first sent me to Koonin, mindful of my having written in the past on cosmic chance in *The Lost Book of Paradise* (1993).

Meanwhile, the evolutionary path leading to Homo sapiens is constantly being repaved. Case in point: we have modernly understood that one of our human markers was the sexual innovation known as the missionary position. However, African lowland gorillas, coming millions of years before us, have now been documented as missionary position specialists (thanks to a Smithsonian filming project). I don't know if any of the surviving great apes will accompany the human ape explorers into deep space in the future or how meager our Noah's ark will look in comparison to the diversity imagined by the Genesis poet. Nevertheless, each animal and plant on earth is an ark unto itself, harboring a multitude of codependent species within.

More than that, we are each a library of life, documenting its history back to the origin. Evolutionary scientists like Koonin can read it back to 'the process of virus-host interaction [in which] viral genes might be left behind and incorporated into the host genome, or host genes might be taken up by viruses and become integrated into the viral genome'. Will such evolutionary knowledge save us? The 'might be's' in Koonin's sentence are a marker for chance, and I'd bet on a poet's prior interpretation, Mallarme's 'Un Coup de des' (1897): 'Un Coup de dés jamais n'abolira le hasard' ('A roll of the dice/ never will abolish/ chance' – trans. J. Clark and R. Bononno, 2015). Still, chance has no choice but to play within the poem of evolution.

# Two Poems

## NED DENNY

## Arrest

*after Chénier*

When the death-cave of the dark abattoir
     Gapes wide for a bleating sheep,
The shepherds and dogs, the slow flock, the far
     Fields are unaware as sleep.
The children who loved his leaps on the green,
     And the rose-complexioned girls
That showered kisses on his face so clean,
     Daisy-chaining those white curls,
Shall now – without one tender thought – praise stew;
     Buried in this living hell,
I have, dumb brother, the same fate as you
     At oblivion's hotel.

Forgotten like me in a house of pain,
     Thousands more blonde sheep will be
Skewered from arsehole to recusant brain
     And served to 'democracy'.
What could my fellow thought-criminals do?
     Yes, lines passed through the black grille
Might salve my dry soul like an April dew...
     Would *gold* assuage them who kill?
But day's now a prison yard; you were right
     To choose life. Friends, stroll at ease,
Be unwilling to take this road in spite
     Of your vanished liberties;
Perhaps in innocent, ignorant years
     I turned my own heedless heart
From the sight of some naked beast in tears.
     Live, citizens, live; be *smart*.

23 March 2020

## Delfica

*after Gérard de Nerval*

Do you know, Daphne, an old song that tells men –
beneath the white laurel, the olive tree, or
the willow, the myrtle, the tall sycamore –
how love is forever beginning again?

Remember the Temple, its vast peristyle,
the bitter lemons in which you bit your mark,
and, fatal to careless intruders, the dark
where there drowses the seed of the great reptile?

Golden days shall be reawakened at last;
the high gods will return, healing your sorrow;
the whole earth has shuddered with prophecy's blast...

meanwhile the classical face of the sibyl,
below Constantine's arch, is slumbering still –
and nothing disturbs that severe portico.

# The Fools and other poems
## LUCY TUNSTALL

## The Fools

The way they walked to church over the fields and made everything milk white.
The way the heat-haze took them out by the ankles and that cloud of white
hair that could actually have *been* cloud. The way they swam in and out
of sight like a pair of stupid moons behind clouds, a kind of cut-out
flatness that made you want to push them all the way over
and drive a steamroller over them real slow.

## Machine

I married a machine that could reconfigure itself. The machine
survived everything. The function of the machine was to burn fuel.

The machine made everything machine-brand – machine-brand
coffee, machine-brand daisies, machine-brand duvet-cover.

My eyes were very heavy when I looked at the machine. To me
the machine looked like a machine, but to other people it looked
like other things.

Parts of the machine were vintage to show originality. The vintage
parts went *oompah oompah* and steam came out and a whistle blew.

The machine turned me into paper and folded me up and pretended
to eat me. The machine rubbed my legs until they were purple
plasticine worms.

I teetered on a little dot of plasticine toe. It was okay.
I went *dot-dot-dot* when I walked away.

## Machine and Lamb

When machine was a little machine

machine had a train set with an engine you could crash. It
would come apart with the insides showing. You could
crash it again and again.

It was meant to be a replica of the Great Tay Bridge Train
Disaster of 1879.

When machine was a piece of art, he was a grand piano
hung upside down from the ceiling, with clattering teeth.

When machine went on holiday, he had to buy a whole
row of seats on the aeroplane because of the unravelling.

Sometimes machine left bits of himself in different places
or as a trail of bent metal behind him as he moved.

When machine was a car crash, he was a car crash.

Some people liked parts of machine, but no one liked
machine in toto.

Machine was never a river.
Machine was never a lamb.
But there *is* a lamb.

Machine has sent the lamb far away where his mother will
never find him because

machine has designs upon lamb
with his soft ears and his velvet bleatings.

'Get away over that farthest hill where I can never find
you.'

Machine was always lost and dusty.
Machine forgot bits of himself, pieces of iron.

When machine went on a self-help retreat, they said to
machine, 'You've forgotten your *purpose*. What are you *for*?
What is your *service*? For what reason were you *created?*'

Hub caps on the pavement.
Rivets in the sink.

Machine has a long list of complaints which he succours
and for which there is no medicine:

fatigue
corrosion
unstable geometry.

And every type of failure: shape, size, material, structure,
load.

Machine has bowing walls and smoke at the mortar joints,
vibrations of gusset and girder, brittle fractures, boiler
explosions.

When machine played the guitar the strings went ping, the
neck shattered. 'Oh machine!' we said, ex-as-per-*ate*-ed-ly.
.
He said it was all part of it; it was dangerous and intriguing.

Machine, I didn't know you could speak. 'Well,' he said, 'I
c...a...n, but only pre-records, so...'

Crankshaft, levers,
eye holes, pistons.

Where is lamb, machine?

What have you done with him?

Machine makes a scraping noise.
Machine doesn't like that question.

# Redressers Dressed Down

## RICARDO NIRENBERG

I have never taught poetry and would have no idea how to go about it. I remember reading J. M. Coetzee's novel *Disgrace* almost twenty years ago and blessing my luck for having made me a teacher of math instead. It seemed patent to me that David Lurie, Coetzee's central character, had brought disgrace upon himself mainly out of frustrations of a pedagogical rather than of a sexual nature. This fifty-year old professor of Romantic Poetry who, for as long as he could remember, carried the harmonies of Wordsworth's *The Prelude* in his heart, asked his student Melanie Isaacs what she thought of the great poet, and the girl could only say:

'Maybe by the end of the course I'll appreciate him more. Maybe he'll grow on me.' 'Maybe,' said Lurie, 'but in my experience poetry speaks to you either at first sight or not at all. A flash of revelation and a flash of response. Like lightning. Like falling in love.'

Then he invited the girl for a drink, and disaster ensued. How can you teach something that speaks to you either at first sight or not at all? Would you tell the class: for next week, read such and such a poem, and see if you get a buzz out of it? How different math: here, whatever you touch upon and no matter the student's first reaction, a good teacher can lead on to subtler points or more surprising consequences, so that a student can fall in love with a theory or a theorem not at first sight but after careful consideration.

I am not saying that I agree with Coetzee's Professor Lurie for, again, I have never taught poetry, and can only say that if Lurie's views are correct, his job was a grim affair. My own linguistic experience as a child was primarily in Spanish, and I carried in my heart the harmonies of the Romancero. As an illustration of the hardships I imagine involved in the teaching of poetry, I'll use the four lines near the end of the Second Part of *Don Quixote*, and more particularly, the first two of those four, in which his quill, now otiose, warns everyone not to touch it – not to presume to write another sequel to the noble and ridiculous story. Those lines:

*Tate, tate, folloncicos / de ninguno sea tocada,*

rang in my childish brain with the force of enchantment. They still do. But if I try to explain why, I run into serious problems. I look it up in several English translations: 'Beware ye cowards, stay your hands! Let it (sic) be touched by none!' Or, 'Hold off! ye weaklings; hold your hands! Adventure it let none!' And two recent ones: 'Careful, careful, worthless idlers!' and 'Hands off, hands off, you paltry knaves!' Paltry indeed, paltry them all. Or the nineteenth-century French translation by Louis Viardot: 'Halte-là, halte-là, félons!' Part of the problem is the almost total absence of diminutives in English and in French, while Spanish is so rich in them. With that in mind I look into an Italian translation: 'Piano, piano, vanerelli! / Da nessuno io sia toccata.' The second line is spoiled by one too many syllables, but 'piano, piano' is much closer to the original 'tate, tate' in meaning, and infinitely better than 'hands off,' 'hold off', or 'stay your hands'. Yet 'tate, tate' is more expressive than 'piano, piano'. It is more gestural, and more specific. 'Vanerelli' is a diminutive alright, but it fails to translate 'folloncicos', little 'follones': 'vano' or 'vain' is not even close to Spanish 'follón', which means, or rather meant back in the seventeenth century, something like French 'félon', a faithless traitor, but *also* a worthless coward – and a noiseless fart. To my childish mind an all too precise instance of 'folloncicos' were the bullies at my school, the boys-only elementary school on Calle Varela (which, incidentally, Pope Francis also attended): you had to be always vigilant, for at the slightest distraction those bullies would touch your tush. Oh well, I could go on and on, and never finish explaining what '*Tate, tate, folloncicos, de ninguno sea tocada*' does for me. It's like trying to explain why I am moved by a dream I dreamt last night: it would require tracing back and forth countless connections to other memories and dreams of mine, old and new, which would exhaust the most patient reader long before it exhausts me too. Math is so much simpler.

Now, would it occur to you to perorate in defence of dreaming? I don't mean it metaphorically, as in so many pop songs, or in 'the American dream': I mean dreaming while one is asleep. Many people say that they never dream, or that they never remember dreaming when they wake; this does not appear to bother them in the least. Perhaps it would be a hindrance if they undertook psychoanalysis, but that is unlikely, what with the abundance of all sort of pills. Even though I find dreaming, as well as poems, important for my life and survival, I would not attempt to convert to dreaming the many who claim they never dream. It would be a fruitless and ridiculous task: quixotic is perhaps the right word. How is it, then, that some distinguished poets take the lectern in what they call a defence or a redress of poetry? Let's try to throw a bit of light on that.

'A Redress of Poetry' is the title of the first of Seamus Heaney's lectures during his tenure as Professor of Poetry at Oxford between 1989 and 1994. It is also the title of the book containing those lectures published by Farrar, Strauss and Giroux in 1995. Right at the beginning of his first lecture, Heaney situates his Redress on the historical line passing through Sir Philip Sidney's *Defence of Poetry* (1595) and Wallace Stevens' essays in *The Necessary Angel* (1951): those are the two landmarks he mentions, and if what we were taught at school is right, two points suffice to determine a straight line uniquely. But is this historical line straight? It looks to me rather crooked. The aim of old apologies of poetry was to defend it against competing disciplines, chiefly Greek philosophy and its proclaimed monopoly on truth. One tried to show, against Plato, that poetry or *mythos* was at least as valuable to the good life and the education of the self as the *logos* and all the *factual* vehicles of ethical instruction and edification. Sidney's *Defence* worked very well in this respect, and this was due to his wit foremost, but also to his remarkable knowledge of the history, philosophy, and poetry of his own time, the Renaissance.

The case with Stevens is different: his essays about the relative merits of facts as against the imagination make little or no sense when viewed from the lookout of twentieth-century thought. Imagination, he says, notoriously (*The Necessary Angel*, Vintage Books, p.36):

> is a violence from within that protects us from a violence without. It is the imagination pressing back against the pressure of reality.

Starting with this polemical antithesis of fact – or 'outside, objective reality' – versus imagination – or 'inner, subjective fiction' – Stevens remains mired in Parmenides' and Plato's fateful distinction between real being and deceptive seeming; between, for instance, a likeness (*eikastikē*) and an illusory image (*phantasma*), in *Sophist* 235d – 236b. The illustrative example the Stranger from Elea gives in Plato's dialogue is colossal statues, in which 'artists, leaving the truth to take care of itself, do in fact put into the images they make, not the *real proportions*, but those that will appear beautiful' (from the perspective of the viewer who is placed near the base of the statue). Pythagoreans and Platonists, it is worth recalling, thought truth to be best (or only) conveyed by numerical proportions. Things have changed. Twentieth-century thinkers are unlikely to agree with a view of imagination such as Stevens', divorced from our notions of reality, and with the untenable distinction between within and without. And hardly likely to agree with what is worse in Stevens' definition: a contentious divorce, a 'violence from within' that pretends to protect us from the violence reality exerts 'without.' Stevens goes on:

> It seems, in the last analysis, to have something to do with our self-preservation; and that, no doubt, is why the expression of it, the sound of its words, helps us to live our lives.

Such is Stevens' apology of poetry, and the first thing that grates our ear is a poor use of rhetoric. He begins dubitatively: 'It seems', without a clear referent to 'It'. The best bet is that it refers to the imagination. So the imagination '*seems*, in the last analysis, to have *something* to do with our self-preservation'. From this wary tentativeness we are suddenly pushed into 'that, *no doubt*, is why ... [it] helps us to live our lives'. From dubious premises to an irrefutable conclusion. And do not pass over Stevens' 'in the last analysis', which may sound like mere padding but is actually a howler. He is talking about imagination and the mind and lays claim to a *last analysis*, without stopping to think that there can be no such thing, no top nor bottom, no beginning nor end, to any inquiry or talk about imagination and the mind.

In the last analysis, my friend, there is no last analysis. See Heraclitus, the earliest psychologist, the first who wrote the words *psyche* and *logos* in the same sentence (fragment B45):

> Whoever goes in search of the boundaries of the psyche will not find them, even after traveling all roads: so deep is its logos.

Stevens, though, in well-known passages of his poems, is pleased to place 'the spirit's base' at the Irish Cliffs of Moher, and to speak of 'The palm at the end of the mind, / Beyond the last thought'.

I am not qualified to talk about, far less criticize, Stevens' poems. My wrestling, like Jacob's, is with his 'necessary angel'. Even so, some might find my qualms impertinent and feel that they do not affect the effectiveness of Stevens' defence of poetry. Should they read further into his essay, however, and turn to page 142, they may be flummoxed by this:

> And I say that the world is lost to him [the poet], certainly, because, for one thing, the great poems of heaven and hell have been written and the great poem of the earth remains to be written.

Should we try to extract some sense from the above? The world is lost to the poet, he says and reinforces it by 'certainly'. Weird reinforcement in what is supposed to be a defence of poetry. Stevens' world seems to be composed of two parts: one is heaven and hell, and the earth is the other. How those two parts interact, if at all, is a question we will not tackle here. The great poems dealing with the part of heaven and hell, he says, have already been written: he may be thinking of Dante's *Commedia* above all, and of other poems of the past, including Milton and perhaps Blake; he seems to be saying, too, that the modern poet should not bother with *that* part of the world or try to add to the old treasures. The modern poet should, it seems, concentrate on the earth, since 'the great poem of the earth remains to be written'. Yet, instead of encouraging the modern poet to get ready, to go ahead and write the poem of the earth, he states, flat out, that 'the world is lost to him'. That's a tough nut to crack, and even tougher is Stevens' statement about the absence, in his own time, of *a* great poem of the earth (let's ignore his definite article, which raises toughness to an impossible degree). But wait. Is he sitting at the top of Mount Parnassus, surveying with unerring ears all lyres and laurel wreaths around, in all human languages? A contemporary of Stevens, after all, did publish in 1923, some twenty-six years before the publication of Stevens' essay, a work richly deserving the name of a great poem of the earth which is, simultaneously, a vigorous defence of poetry: I mean Rilke's *Sonnets to Orpheus*. I'll indulge in just one peek. Read Sonnet I.11 (last tercet):

> "Auch die sternische Verbindung trügt,
> Doch uns freue eine Weile nun,
> der Figur zu glauben. Das genügt."
> (Even the starry connection is deceiving.

Yet we enjoy it for a while,
  believing in the figure. That's enough.)

Here we have Rilke's reply to Plato's opposition between likeness (*eikastikē*) and an illusory image (*phantasma*). The starry connection we call Orion (let us choose it as our example) has been identified in the oldest cave paintings: we have believed in it and we have enjoyed it, I'd say, for quite a while. Surely, it is only our take on a bunch of stars – Rigel, Betelgeuse and others – hugely distant from one another and from us, from our hugely particular, minuscule abode and point of view on this earth. And so, from any Platonic perspective, it is a lie: *es trügt*. Yet, as Rilke affirms, it suffices, *es genügt*. And in this rhyme we find the music that brings our puny lives into harmony with truth.

But to return to Stevens: readers who are not baffled enough by our quote from page 142 of *The Necessary Angel* should go on reading some lines down, where our essayist impersonates Napoleon in his declaration to Goethe, 'Today, politics is fate':

One wants to consider the imagination on its most momentous scale. Today this scale is not the scale of poetry, nor of any form of literature or art. It is the scale of international politics and in particular of communism. Communism is not the measure of humanity. But I limit myself to an allusion to it as a phenomenon of the imagination. Surely the diffusion of communism exhibits imagination on its most momentous scale. With the collapse of other beliefs, this grubby faith promises a practicable earthly paradise.

Stevens was not a communist. He is considering communism as 'a phenomenon of the imagination', 'a grubby faith' that moves millions. In 1949, after the great war in which fascists and Nazis were defeated, at the time when China was turning red, communism indeed appeared as a formidable faith that moved millions, and that faith is what Stevens calls 'imagination on its most momentous scale'. This provides a clue to Stevens' notion of imagination as something admitting of a measuring scale, a momentous one no less, like a huge majority in a political election; an imagination identified with a *faith* in an earthly paradise in the teeth of a manifest inversion of paradise and hell, an imagination that *promises* rather than simply *presents* to our mind, as insight and reason blessedly and never demagogically do. Which harks to that earlier, romantic notion of imagination in Wordsworth's *The Prelude*, Professor Lurie's favourite poem:

  This spiritual Love acts not nor can exist
  Without Imagination, which, in truth,
  Is but another name for absolute power
  And clearest insight, amplitude of mind,
  And Reason in her most exalted mood.

Neither pressure nor violence here, no promises, but light, insight. I take 'absolute power' to mean that imagination is not curtailed by logical principles like identity or non-contradiction: it goes 'all the way down', as

Richard Rorty writes in his *Philosophy As Poetry*. Stevens, though, doesn't miss an opportunity to pooh-pooh the romantics:

The imagination is one of the great human powers. Romanticism belittles it. The imagination is the liberty of the mind. The romantic is a failure to make use of that liberty. It is to the imagination what sentimentality is to feeling. It is a failure of the imagination precisely as sentimentality is a failure of feeling. (p.138)

Perhaps when he talked of the Romantics poets such as Wordsworth were far from his mind? Was Stevens influenced by his teacher George Santayana, who in his Introduction to *The Life of Reason* wrote: 'The historian of reason should not be a romantic poet, vibrating impotently to every impulse he finds afoot, without a criterion of excellence or a vision of perfection?' Hard to say. Yet, assuming that Stevens knew what he was talking about when he attacked romanticism, for nothing in the world would I miss the chance to point out that his notion of imagination as a pressure from within opposing a pressure from without, a push and shove between the I and the not-I, owes, physically, of course, to Newton's Third Law, but philosophically speaking, more to J. G. Fichte than to anybody else. Most likely Fichte was on the syllabus when young Stevens was studying philosophy at Harvard. On the other hand, Fichte and his push and shove between I and not-I were foundational for the early, the Jena Romantics: for Hölderlin and for Novalis, for the Schlegel brothers, and for Ludwig Tieck, the translator of *Don Quixote*. In a recent article by Henrik S. Wilberg, I learn that the German word *Thathandlung* that Tieck uses to translate Cervantes' *hazaña* (great deed) is a Fichtean coinage.

One should like to say, then, that there is a basic contradiction between Stevens' Fichtean notion of the imagination and his belittling of Romanticism; yet 'contradiction' is not the right word, for contradictions are often fruitful, as Fichte himself realized in his notion, later played up by Hegel, of synthesis of contraries. No, contradictions are not the problem with Stevens' discourse on imagination and poetry: the problem is rather its slipperiness. Take his dictum, 'Surely the diffusion of communism exhibits imagination on its most momentous scale', which we quoted a moment ago; I took the trouble to explain the confusion in that statement, pointing out that the imagination is not about promises of earthly paradises, or any other sort of promises; only to read, a paragraph on:

The difference between an imagination that is engaged by the materialism of communism and one that is engaged by the projects of idealism is a difference in nature. It is not that the imagination is versatile but that there are different imaginations.

Oh, I see. And the imagination engaged by American pragmatism is still another, of a different nature. And so is the imagination engaged by mathematics, etc. So I am wasting my time trying to confute what Stevens says about imagination in one paragraph, since in the following paragraph he will be dealing with a different imagination. It is like pouncing on an annoying fly, and squashing it, only to find that now a similar but different fly is annoying you.

But it so happens that near the end of his essay, 'Imagination as Value' (p.153), Stevens finally provides a general definition, or so we hope, of imagination:

My final point, then, is that the imagination is the power that enables us to perceive the normal in the abnormal, the opposite of chaos in chaos.

Vain hope. As soon as we start munching on this one, we notice that, first, to perceive the normal in the abnormal seems to be the function of a very different power, that of habituation; and then, that to perceive the opposite of chaos (symmetries? order or form, perhaps?) in chaos looks like the Rorschach inkblot test, in which, if I am not mistaken, it is the power of hidden emotions that is tested. Are those powers 'different imaginations', *d'après* Stevens? I don't know. All I know is that I find all those different takes, distinctions, and classifications unhelpful. Worse yet, this slovenly and slippery intellectual style may be contagious. In her short book, *Wallace Stevens: Words Chosen Out of Desire* (1984), Helen Vendler begins by balancing Stevens among her favourites:

Though there are poets undeniably greater than Stevens, and poets whom I love as well, he is the poet whose poems I would have written had I been the poet he was.

I take that to mean that had she been a poet at the level of Stevens, Vendler believes she would have written poems much like his. But how could she know that? Had she become a poet at the level of Stevens, that metamorphosis by itself would have meant that her other remarkable powers would have changed too. That, at least, I find likely, or, if you wish, 'natural'. But it seems that here, for once, Vendler has bought into Stevens' clockwork notions about human faculties – one for imagining a communist paradise, another for imagining a Platonic heaven of Forms and contemplation, perhaps another for hell, chaos, and torments, another for small things, still another for large ones, yet another for vermicular shapes, and it goes on and on (see p.143 of Steven's *The Necessary Angel*) – and, the oddest, the most remarkable property of those faculties is that each is independent from the others, so that any one of them can be transformed without affecting the rest.

Leaving Stevens' angel for now, we go back to Seamus Heaney, our original redresser of poetry, and to his book. After paying homage to Stevens' violence from within to counter the unavoidable violence from without, Heaney reaches out for Simone Weil. From a this-worldly mind to one who yearned for disembodied transcendence: anything may be of help in the noble and ridiculous cause of the defence of poetry, even two oddballs whose arguments, if examined with detachment, should lead to a dismissal of their value as defence, or worse, might lead to a condemnation of poetry.

The book by Weil, *La Pesanteur et la grâce* (*Gravity and Grace*, translated by Emma Crawford and Mario von der Ruhr), was put together and published by Gustave Thibon in 1947, four years after Weil's death; it opens with the following opposition between natural and supernatural:

All the *natural* movements of the soul are controlled by laws analogous to those of physical gravity. Grace is the only exception. We must always expect things to happen in conformity with the laws of gravity unless there is supernatural intervention.

This is an egregious case of begging the question. Anything that falls under physical laws – meaning that it is subject to the principle of sufficient reason or sufficient cause, and subject to the strictures of mathematics (the identity principle and the principle of non-contradiction) – is called 'natural'. To Simone Weil, steeped since childhood more into math than into Christianity, that seemed, well, natural. But a great many psychic phenomena are not natural *that way*, since they cannot be assigned a sufficient cause and cannot be quantified. Think of these lines by Pedro Salinas, the twentieth-century Spanish poet:

Y súbita, de pronto,
porque sí, la alegría.
(And suddenly, unannounced
for no reason, here's joy).

If we follow Weil, Salina's joy is grace, it is supernatural. And indeed, the poet calls it 'gracia' and 'dádiva' (gift) a few lines on, but, I dare say, metaphorically. The psyche does not follow physical laws, as we already heard from Heraclitus. What Weil does is to assign that vast domain of psychic everyday life to the rule of grace and the supernatural. For her there is math and there is divine grace, and that's it: nothing else, a gaping void in between. The distant echo of Nicolas Malebranche and his occasionalism rings in the mind, and more resoundingly, that of still another Frenchman, Louis-Ferdinand Céline, who had expressed a somewhat similar, equally crazy idea, in his 1932 *Voyage au but de la nuit*:

Entre le pénis et les mathématiques, il n'existe rien ! Rien ! (Between the penis and mathematics there is nothing! Nothing!)

Enough said about Weil's ontology. The remainder of her book deals with the old problem of how to make ourselves open to divine grace. A phrase inscribed on a portal of the Romanesque Basílica de San Vicente in Ávila, the hometown of a famous female saint, reads: 'Para subir al cielo, se sube siempre bajando.' (To ascend to heaven, one ascends by going always down.) The medieval recipe is taken over by Weil in a peculiar way: instead of going always down one must make oneself into a void, and for this it is essential to *stop* all imagination:

'Grace fills empty spaces but it can only enter where there is a void to receive it, and it is grace itself which makes this void.' (p.10) 'The imagination, filler up of the void, is essentially a liar.' (p.16) 'In no matter what circumstances, if the imagination is stopped from pouring itself out we have a void (the poor in spirit).' (p.17) 'All sins are attempts to fill voids.' (p.24). 'A man attempts suicide, recovers and is no more detached afterwards than he was before. His suicide was imaginary. Suicide is probably never anything else, and that is why it is forbidden.' (p.51–2) 'How can we distinguish the imaginary from the real in the spiritual realm? We must prefer real hell to an imaginary paradise.' (p.53) 'What comes to us from Satan is our imagination.' (p.54). And so relentlessly, dismally on...

Leaving aside this divine grace that works much like a gas, a noble one to be sure, who can possibly use Weil's manic lucubration's against imagination as a defence of poetry? No one. Yet Seamus Heaney does. He cheats, since most of what he takes from her book is not what she had to say about the imagination and its evils but something else, which happens not to be in her book properly speaking at all. It is in the Introduction by Gustave Thibon, the man who received Simone's large pack of notes before she and her family left for the USA in 1942, from which notes he put the book together. On page xvii of the Introduction Thibon explains:

It was thus that, in spite of her dislike for Communism, she [Simone] wanted to go to Russia when that country was bleeding under the heel of the Germans.

Immediately comes the text Heaney quotes:

This idea of *counterbalancing* is essential in her [Simone's] conception of political and social activity: 'If we know in what direction the scales of society are tilted we must do what we can to add weight to the lighter side. ... We must have a conception of equal balance and be always ready to change sides like Justice – that fugitive from the camp of conquerors.'

Heaney adds to the above text of Thibon his own sanctimonious historical remark: 'Clearly, this corresponds to deep structures of thought and feeling derived from centuries of Christian teaching and from Christ's paradoxical identification with the plight of the wretched.'

I'd say this ideal of Weil's, balancing and counterbalancing, owes more to the ancient Greeks than to Christianity. All the way from the Delphic inscription, *mēdèn ágan* (nothing in excess), to Archimedes' mathematical exploits in finding areas and volumes by counterbalancing bits and pieces, passing through the addiction of the classical Greek language for the balancing particles *men* and *de*. Christian teachings, in spite of Heaney's opinions and as far as I can tell, are not generally concerned with counterbalancing the bliss of the fortunate with the plight of the wretched. A powerful example of such unconcern, or rather of a will to deepen the ditch between plight and bliss, is the coexistence, in Christian teaching, of Paradise and Hell. Nietzsche attributed it to *resentment*. But neither Heaney nor Weil appear to remember Nietzsche; from the correspondence with her brother André I gather that Simone refused to read *The Genealogy of Morals* and *Beyond Good and Evil*: her bal-

ancing act did not go that far. As for Heaney, whether he remembered such things or not, whether or not he ever thought of them, he went mindlessly on the high-wire and recruited Weil's counterbalancing for his Redress:

And in the activity of poetry, too, there is a tendency to place a counter-reality in the scales – a reality which may be only imagined but which nevertheless has weight because it is imagined with the gravitational pull of the actual and can therefore hold its own and balance out against the historical situation.

This imagination which, together with gravitation, are, according to Weil, the veritable scandal and the chief obstacle to our receptivity of divine grace, here become, by sleight of mind, the alliance at the heart of poetry. Heaney, like Stevens, imagined he was producing a redress; in actual fact, both give occasion for poetry's dismissal and contempt.

What follows may appear paradoxical. A good attack on poetry should give us readers more essential hope, more 'necessary angel', than a poor defence thereof. This is because our essential hope is not hope in the art of poetry, nor in the art of prose, nor in mathematics, or science, or medicine, nor (excuse my unbelief) in divine grace: it is rather hope in, or rather for, whatever is divine or awesome (*deinós*, as Sophocles has it in *Antigone*) in fellow humans, and such hope is kindled by intelligent speech and smothered by silly solemnities. Borges once prayed:

We don't know the designs of the universe, but we do know that lucid reasoning and acting justly help those designs, which will not be revealed to us.

The Polish writer Witold Gombrowicz, who had taken refuge in Argentina in August 1939, rightly raged against the Dantesque inscription on the portal of Hell (*Inferno* 3) pretending that the eternal establishment had been created by divine primal love – the amazing chutzpa! – and he did so as part of a basket of texts he titled 'Against the Poets'. As an attack on poetry, it is a suitable relief and welcome counterbalance to the redressers of poetry who are the ostensible subject of this essay. The contrast between Heaney the poet and Gombrowicz the prose writer is deep. Heaney executed his Redress as Professor of Poetry at Oxford, a world-celebrated poet who had received many prizes and held an endowed professorship at Harvard: he was loaded, lauded, and applauded; Gombrowicz delivered the first version of his 'Against the Poets' in Spanish, a language he did not master, at a book store in Buenos Aires in August 1947, after he had secured a minor job at Banco Polaco which kept hunger and homelessness at bay. When he finished his diatribe, he was jeered and insulted, which of course pleased him. The motive force behind his outburst against the ovates was, as he put it at the outset: an elemental anger triggered in us by any error of style, any falsehood, any flight away from reality.

Czesław Milosz was the only poet, as far as I know, who was Gombrowicz's friend until the end: they held each other in high esteem and admiration, and I wish I had space enough to comment on Milosz's judgment on Gombrowicz the writer in *The Land of Ulro*, for it is germane to our purpose. Nor will I attempt to find out –something others have attempted – what is it that makes great artists coming from that bloodied boundary band between two Christian spirits – 'only from the Father' and 'also from the Son' – deeper than their counterparts from less punished lands. I must comment, however, on Gombrowicz' experience with the crazy book by Simone Weil.

At the beginning of 1956 Gombrowicz was spending a few days at a house in Mar del Plata, the beach resort 400 Km. south of the city of Buenos Aires, and he tells us in his *Diary* (translated by Lillian Vallee) that he was reading Dumas' *Le Vicomte de Bragelonne* and Simone Weil's *La Pesanteur et la grâce*. This sort of balancing act is typical of Gombrowicz: if he's to write about a heavyweight like Weil, he must first tell us that it is 'mandatory reading: I have to write about it for an Argentine weekly', and he must make it clear that for his own pleasure he is reading instead the immensely popular Dumas. The diary entry for Thursday ends with:

> Simone Weil and I are the sharpest contrast that one can imagine, two mutually exclusive interpretations,

two opposing systems. And it is this woman I confront in an empty house, at the very moment when it is so hard to escape from myself.

And the following Sunday, after spilling out his distaste for everything that is 'great', for 'profundity and loftiness', especially for Weil's sort, he sums it all up:

> This greatness loses in contact with commonness, immediately succumbs to a ridiculous dégringolade and what do we see? A hysterical woman, tormenting and boring, an egotist, whose swollen and aggressive personality is incapable of noticing others – a knot of tensions, torments, hallucinations, and manias, something casting about in the external world, like a fish taken out of water, for the real element of this spirit is only its own sauce.

Those denunciations are from Gombrowicz's *Diary*, separated by nine years from his earlier provocations in 'Against the Poets': they manifest the same spirit, the same irreverence and the same elementary anger that pushes me to inveigh against the nonsense of Wallace Stevens and Seamus Heaney when they took up their cudgels in defence of poetry.

# Morning lies along the hill and other poems
## CAROLA LUTHER

## Today is blue like blue used to be

I could almost ignore the fields
pale as sponges, the exhausted trees
stunned but upright

Horses stand side-on to the sun
either asleep or watching steam rise
the whitish grass

Still as tables laid with cloth and bowls
of warm food, they don't move a muscle
They don't want to ruin it

Flowers are tougher
than they look. Crocuses push up
their soft torpedoes and daffodils yell at the sun

Building continues. Bony crow-nests
shake high up, twig and wing
loud on the sky. Trees will remember

It's the beech trees gingerly
hanging out blossom of grey tatty plastic
I want to talk to

Perhaps they and the horses
understand facts I've only half-grasped
Being human I hope

it might go something like this
When we are finished, first them then us
or maybe the other way round

there won't be redemption
exactly, but days of a kind, ugly
and heavenly as this

# Morning lies along the hill

*for SK*

Morning lies along the hill, lover
waking slowly
half-folded in cloud.

Purple and orange haze
balanced on the tips
of Rough Hey wood

has disappeared overnight.
Now trees rediscover
the greens they can be.

I think of you waking
in another house
sunlight your body

stored all through
this bright and lamenting spring
coming off you

a light of your own
that you rest in
and will leave behind.

If I could touch it
the light would be almost
warm as you

following shape
close to the shapes
you have been

as you slept.
Like leaves becoming
just above the woods.

# This May Morning

The sun and the dead
The milkman clock.
On the whispering radio
politics.
Outside, a cat

stalks through vetch.
Buttercups. Quaking-grass.
Son without work.
Everything is attached
to its own leaning shadow.

Alone in your bones
you wake. Our sunlit bed.
This May morning
your years lie on you
strange, heavy coat.

# Chaucer

## ANDREW HADFIELD

Marion Turner, *Chaucer: A European Life*
(Princeton University Press), £34.00

We know a lot more about Chaucer than many of his contemporaries, and writers who lived a considerably long time after him, but, even so, there are huge gaps in the life records. In her splendid new biography, Marion Turner has chosen to 'tell the story of his life and poetry through spaces and places, rather than through strict chronology'. In doing so the aim is to explore his 'imaginative development', and not an emotional life that is 'beyond the biographer's reach' (p.3). It is a useful guideline for lives of writers but runs the obvious danger that the rules have to be bent a bit every now and then. More significantly we might ask what a biography should do. If we cannot access the inner life are we not getting a sophisticated and intimate contextual study? And, if readers compare biographies, ones in which the subject seems more alive, more like a friend, will matter more to them. This might seem like a trivial point but it is surely the case that those writers we can imagine as people will assume a more significant presence than those we cannot.

I raise this issue because I think Prof. Turner has been even more successful than she states, in that she has explained how and why Chaucer developed as a poet, and given us a sense of how he lived and moved through the late Medieval world. Chaucer imagined himself as a European, and we need to remember that he was intimately connected to a world beyond a life largely spent in London. The 'father of English poetry', as John Dryden, another enthusiastic translator, called him, was never a little Englander. He was writing at a time when English was only just becoming widespread as a serious language of law, politics and culture in England, starting to replace French and Anglo-Norman. If we side-line these polyglot origins we distort Chaucer's significance. The iambic pentameter he pioneered may have become quintessentially English but it arrived via Italy and France.

Chaucer came from a family of prosperous London wine merchants and booze features frequently in his writings: the pilgrims in *The Canterbury Tales* are described in terms of alcoholic beverages, and it emboldens the boorish Miller to challenge the Knight in the opening exchange, one in which the lower status man may well come off best. As a youth, Chaucer served in the household of Edward III and Prof. Turner writes with great insight on the king's building projects at Windsor and Westminster in the 1350s and 1360s. Space became a class issue. While those lower down the scale were always in the company of others in communal rooms, the palaces contained far more private, enclosed spaces for the aristocratic inhabitants. Secret conversations, assignations, and affairs were best conducted unobserved, but not everyone had this luxury: 'at court there were regular prostitutes, and presumably it was accepted that sex need not be a private activity' (p.53). Prof. Turner suggests that these hierarchical living conditions influenced the behaviour represented in Chaucer's poetry where sex occurs in a tree and is planned for a garden.

The move from life with merchants to aristocrats would surely have been a social challenge for Chaucer. He would have encountered a wealth of French poetry at court, especially the fashionable verse of poets such as Guillaume de Machaut, whose poems dramatizing the relationship between poets and master undoubtedly influenced one of Chaucer's early poems, *The Book of the Duchess*, written for his long-standing patron, John of Gaunt, after the death of his wife, Blanche, in 1368. It also surely gave him much more to write about, in particular the complicated and often fractious social divisions that structured the upper levels of English society at the time. Then, as now, the court depended on the finance of merchants even though they were regarded as somewhat vulgar. Accordingly, Chaucer represents paradigmatic figures as chalk and cheese. The Merchant in *The Canterbury Tales* is an uneasy figure, bitter and frustrated, he tells a tale that expresses his anxieties and feelings of inferiority. The Knight, on the other hand, is either an aloof, Olympian figure, or a hypocritical psychopath.

Chaucer got to travel with his masters to France and Italy, where he may well have met Petrarch, the European superstar of lyric poetry. But Chaucer would already have been well versed in Italian, as well as French poetry, and Prof. Turner is especially insightful as she argues that the ambitious English upstart, writing in a barbarous language, was prepared to take on the giants of European letters. He loved to change the focus of the works he adopted. While Boccaccio's *Filostrato* shows the characters in the grip of forces they cannot control, Chaucer emphasizes human agency, expanding the role of Pandarus as the initiator of Troilus and Criseyde's affair. For Chaucer people were much more responsible for their actions than they often realized.

Chaucer is an intensely visual poet – one of the reasons why he is enjoyed as well as acknowledged as influential – and Prof. Turner speculates that he may have seen a number of Giotto's innovative paintings while in Florence. Giotto was admired by the poets Chaucer wished to emulate and challenge, Boccaccio and Dante, who represented his art in their works, as well as translating his ideas into verbal form. Chaucer, she suggests, would have been fascinated not just by Giotto's revolutionary use of perspective and light, but by his social politics and connections to the *popolo* who had stared to assert themselves more effectively and challenge the aristocratic elites in Italian city-states.

He would also have witnessed the appalling effects of war in Edward III's campaigns in France, one episode in the protracted Hundred Years War, as a scorched earth policy reduced much of the fertile agricultural land to barren wastelands. Chaucer is a poet who has little time for chivalric nonsense (the Knight really is a psycho) and usually represents violence and war as horrific and senseless, from the increasingly tragic divisions opened up between lovers and families in his masterpiece, *Troilus and Criseyde*, to the extended brutality represented in the stories in *The Monk's Tale* and the lack of honour amongst the murderous thieves in *The Pardoner's Tale*. As Prof. Turner puts it, 'Compromise, not conquest, was Chaucer's forte' (p.94). He was also imprisoned and later ransomed, so it is perhaps no surprise that images of walls and incarceration are commonplace in his poetry. A later chapter shows how Chaucer also frequently represents human life as that of caged animals, probably taken from Boethius's *Consolation of Philosophy*, which he translated.

After his travels, Chaucer was given a lucrative position overseeing accounts in London's Wool Quay, one of a number of posts he secured through the support of the increasingly unpopular John of Gaunt, later the target of mob fury in the Peasants' Revolt of 1381. Chaucer frequently resorts to images of accountancy in his poetry, describing how an accountant has to 'reckon' figures in *The Book of the Duchess* and then representing the Day of Judgement as a 'reckoning' in *The Parson's Tale*. His marriage to Philippa de Roet, Prof. Turner argues, was probably petering out in this period. She was the sister of Katherine Swyneford, John of Gaunt's second wife and of a much higher class than he was. They maintained separate households and seem not to have been especially close and there are no clues of shared affection as there are with Chaucer and his daughter, Elizabeth, and son, Thomas. Chaucer's last sexual relationship, therefore, may have been with Cecily Champaigne, one that led to a charge of rape, 'the most controversial of all the life records' (p.211). Prof. Turner argues that rape really did mean rape here, not, as some critics have argued, abduction, and it may have been the result of a relationship that went disastrously wrong and ended in non-consensual sexual activity. Chaucer paid off his accuser and the case was dropped.

Chaucer's intellectual enthusiasms were wide and various. He was interested in astronomy, writing a treatise on the astrolabe, at the cutting edge of technological development in the late fourteenth century, as it enabled sailors to travel much further than they ever had done before. Astronomy and ability to read the stars features in a number of tales, sometimes used for nefarious purposes as in *The Miller's Tale* when the student, Nicholas, bamboozles the gullible John into thinking he has knowledge of the imminent end of the world through his observations of the heavens so he [John] can sleep with his wife. Chaucer was also keen on the theory, practice, and history of gardens, demonstrated in his translation of the unfinished allegorical *Roman de la Rose*, as well as *The Parliament of Fowls*.

As a mature writer Chaucer appears to have been fascinated by the legends of the fall of Troy, in particular the contrast between the 'attractive surface' of Trojan social life with 'dinner parties, books groups, and festivals', and the undercurrents of 'political and personal betrayals, secret stratagems, intimations of rape' (p.271), an image of life, perhaps, in Ricardian London. Chaucer, unlike his contemporary John Gower, hardly writes about the Peasants' Revolt, only mentioning it in *The Nun's Priest's Tale* as a metaphor for farmyard chaos. But, as a resident in London with links to the relatively new king, Richard II, he would have been unable to avoid its terrifying impact, especially given the hostility to John of Gaunt, whose London palace was burned down. The image of Troy in *Troilus and Criseyde* is that of a 'city of treachery, a city that self-destructs' (p.272), may be one explanation for the rebellion, as well as the power struggle in the city afterwards between the elite oligarchy and the city's less powerful citizens. Chaucer did not seem to have much time for aristocrats and generally sided with those who were not born to power and privilege. *The Parliament of Fowls*, one of his most sophisticated shorter poems and one which features frequently through the biography, aims some pointed barbs at contemporary parliaments, as the 'leisurely debate between aristocrats, structured by endless repetition and conventional language, is interrupted by the strident voices of the lower classes' (p.301), eager to get the debate moving. One of the great innovations of Chaucer's poetry is that he has a balanced and fair understanding that a variety of voices, including those of many different women and those from the less privileged classes, need to have equal footing with aristocratic men.

Chaucer was republican-esque in spirit, and was scornful of over-mighty rulers, one reason for his antagonistic as well as respectful rivalry with his Italian counterparts. Petrarch was supported by the Visconti family in Milan, who mixed a reverence for art and culture with brutal and brutish exploitation of the city's citizens. He may have had more leisure to write than Chaucer but 'was deeply compromised as the client of tyrants' (p.326). For Chaucer Italian verse was both intellectually liberating and politically troubling. In *The House of Fame* he takes on another brilliant poet who was prepared to do the bidding of autocratic regimes, Dante. Chaucer's poem works best as a parody of the *Paradiso*, his unstoppable, garrulous eagle set against Dante's imperial bird, his notion of the random and chaotic human origins of poetry working against Dante's faith in 'divine inspiration and destiny' (p.338). While Dante believed in the power of one voice speaking the truth, Chaucer preferred to exist in a cacophonous world, that was at heart 'radically egalitarian' (p.364). He was also, unlike Dante, a poet who revelled in the unfinished, works without endings.

Of course, this sense of equality is most obviously demonstrated in *The Canterbury Tales*, which has proved more popular with readers than *Troilus and Criseyde*, even if not as sustained a masterpiece, in part because of its agreeable disorder and diversity. This radical approach to writing leads to the clever intermingling and subverting of genres so that the opening fragment of the tales shows us that romance and fabliaux both use the same plots. Later, in the Wife of Bath's prologue and tale

Chaucer actively encourages readers to challenge and even overthrow the authorities that have dominated Western culture in their demeaning representation of women. As Prof. Turner comments at the end of her reading, the tale forcefully 'puts forward the position that women and men of all ages and estates are moral equivalents' (p.464), a vision appropriate for the writer who sired modern English literature.

Well-written, engaging, learned, critically astute throughout, *Chaucer: A European Life* shows how and why Chaucer matters. It is a big, serious book that wears its learning lightly and is never dull. Chaucer emerges as a complicated, flawed, very human figure, eager to be fair to everyone, but not always managing it. When Prof. Turner outlines her varied perceptions of Chaucer on the last page she has truly earned the right to share them with the reader:

When I think of Chaucer, I think about the boy in fashionable skin-tight leggings and paltok; the man riding across the snowy mountains to multicultural Navarre; the experimental poet who thought he'd try adding extra syllables to his poetic line; the father ... who wrote a scientific tract for his son and visited his daughter in her nunnery... the traveller in Italy, devouring manuscripts in a Pavian library (p.508).

# Red Cities and other poems
## MARYAM HESSAVI

## Red Cities

I came to this planet earth
with cherries hanging on my ears

and I was not a girl.
I am also that girl.

I followed the path of the horse's gallop,
by a setar that played without strings

and I was not a musician. I am
also that hand that plays. The man

dropped a coin for my sound.
I am that man. The glint rolled as sound

loaded a horn so loud it banged
and worth was fashioned   well. I am

a bursted eardrum. The ear felt
wind  sigh past. Wind cuts across

the ear. That ear is me.
The ear is a house that rests

on water with stilts that wobble.
Those stilts are me. And that house

belongs to me. Mine is my name
and my body. The body is

me     where no maps are drawn.
The pencil belongs to me. I am

the belonger, and he is mine and me. Mine
is a home of cherry trees and they are

sharpened. I am the stone from one
eaten. That meal is me and I kneel

before the mouth that does.
Teeth are me. Gums.

The tongue  is enough.
I am taste buds and they

flower an orchard every June.
I am June. My Mother is Joon.

Joon is a place over  bitter seas.
I am that. I do not sail past  blue lines.

*joon, meaning 'dear' in Farsi*

*Note*
'Red Cities' was originally written for
*Poets and Players'* 2019 Poetry Commission:
'Reimagining the City'.

## Sepideh

There is a small village near Shiraz, cracking
by the mountains' foot, pinning down

earth. There  is a girl, she has letters
which she speaks to Einstein through,

translated into stars. She has been banned
from standing  in the mountain's palm  at night

by her mahram, who has  no  or little time. She
has married a man with a PhD

so she can fly  far, to the US, to study
constellations. Anousheh invited her. *Dige*


*\* dige / another*

## Abdul

Seventeen sacks
of rice grain came
pouring on his toes     he'd
stabbed each pack stacked
on the shelves that lined a wall along
the back part of his father's shop: Patel's

angry            at the lies people can tell
                 all about him  were
                 mad clouds   of
*Paki* of *Camel-Carter* of *Dirty
Arab* of *Terrorist
Cell* of
        *Radicalization*
        all
floating round his face
and beard

but now:
the cool slide
of off-white rice
                        falling
            down his
        open ankles;
Rolling
 down the skin on
        phalanges in-between
         his toes and
         filling  up towards these clouds,
felt
   like  dry ablution.

Struck here     to this hard ground he
curled his toes through
                these
                bits of heaven rising,
        cold silk
                up his shins,

he could stand here for a long time
                and speak
                        think
        only    ever
        pearl rice.

# Hunger Strikes (Broken Sequence)

## VICTORIA KENNEFICK

### 1. Hunger Strikes Catherine of Siena (1347–1380)

My sister taught me how.
Oh Bonaventura, they wanted
me to marry him, the slack-jawed widower.

I vomited twigs, hid in the convent,
wore a widow's habit. The other nuns complained
until at twenty-one I met Him.

He presented me with a ring fashioned from His skin.
Told me this sliver of flesh bound us,
wait, He told me, promising it would be special.

I levitated; only ate His body, others did not
understand how good it was
to kiss His holy prepuce.

Oh, Bonaventura, I am a house of sticks,
my bones rattle with desire until I lick it.
I feel it quiver, alive on my tongue.

### 2. Hunger Strikes Angela of Foligno (1248–1309)

I drink pus from wounds of the unclean.
Christ, it is like water to me, sweet
as the Eucharist.
                    I pick
                    at their scabs, chew them flat
                    between my teeth.
The lice I pluck and let drown
on my tongue sustain me.
Lord, I am the Host.
                    Lead me in the light
                    to the summit of perfection.
                    I will pray and pray
and pray to you: to remain poor,
be obedient, chaste and humble.
This is all I ask. God-man, feed me.

### 3. Hunger Strikes Veronica Giuliani (1660–1727)

My confessor ordered her to do it,
the novice kicked me again and again.

Her shoe pummelled my teeth,
bloodied my lips. I did not stir
or whimper, I kept my mouth open.

I remained bruised for weeks.

When my face was almost pink again
He prompted me to clean the walls and floor

of my cell with my tongue. I licked
for hours, scraping up each wisp of skin and hair.
My throat became thick with cobwebs,

my mind clear as light.

### 4. Hunger Strikes Columba of Rieti (1467–1501)

My body is a temple I keep
clean for You, spotless –
lashing my skin so it grows

tired of bleeding.
Wearing hair shirts I cannot forget
what it means to be alert.

I have toured the Holy Land in visions.
I don't imagine they would understand
what I see.

When they came for me, the men,
they ripped off my robes
expecting to find me virginal,

untouched.
How they gasped in horror!
How glad I was that I had used myself

like an old rag.
Beating myself with that spiked
chain shielded me,

my breasts and hips so deformed
they ran from me,
screaming.

*5. Hunger Strikes Gemma Galgani (1878–1903)*

Chapter 1:    St. Gemma's Birth and Early Education:
              First Flowers of Virtue. Her Mother's Death

Chapter 2:    St. Gemma's life at Home.
              Her Heroic Patience in Great Trials

Chapter 3:    St. Gemma's Dangerous Illness and
              Miraculous Recovery

Chapter 4:    St. Gemma Tries to Enter Religion.
              She is Not Received

Chapter 5:    St. Gemma Receives the Stigmata

Chapter 6:    St. Gemma Meets the Passionist Fathers.
              More About the Stigmata

Chapter 7:    St. Gemma's Characteristic Virtue

Chapter 8:    The Means by Which St. Gemma Attained
              Perfection. First, her Detachment

Chapter 9:    St. Gemma's Perfect Obedience

Chapter 10: St. Gemma's Profound Humility

Chapter 11: St. Gemma's Heroic Mortification

Chapter 12: Attacks by the Devil[1]

Chapter 13: St. Gemma's Gift is Raised on the Wings
              of Contemplation to the Highest Degree
              of Divine Love[2]

Chapter 14: St. Gemma's Last Sickness[3]

Chapter 15: St. Gemma's Death and Burial[4]

*6. Hunger Strikes Victoria Kennefick*

She punches her stomach loose, blind –
naked like a baby mole.
In the shower she cannot wash herself clean
the way she'd like. Rid herself
of useless molecules. Would that she
could strip her bones,
be something
neat,
complete.
Useful.

To eat or not to eat,
switch table sides.
Stuff cheese sandwiches
and chocolate blocks into a wide
moist orifice. Or, alternatively
zip that mouth
closed like a jacket,
a body already
contained within.
It doesn't need
to feed.

*But I have set a table for us all.*
*For us all, a feast!*
*On a vast, smooth cloth, already soiled.*
*Let's take a seat, eat our fill.*
*You know you want to,*
*dig in.*

**Notes**

1 All night I dream of food, Jesus take my taste from me. Rip out my tongue and I will explate,
  through my bleeding for you, all the sins committed by your shrouded men.
2 For sixty days I vomited whenever I ate.
3 I was tormented by banquets.
4 Am I threatened by flesh or its opposite?

# Researching the Irish Famine

\*

Bulldozers disturb the old workhouse site,
uncover babies' skulls
curved like tiny moons. Their mothers
beside them, lullabies
locked in their jaws.

\*

They can measure hunger now. Test
how much bellies rumbled, the stress
teeth were under, rotten
before they broke
scurvied gums.

\*

Mothers exhausted their own bodies
to produce milk. High nitrogen
evidence of body tissue
breaking down,
recycling.

\*

The starving
human
literally
consumes
itself.

\*

Babies died
anyway. They all died. Wasted away
like potatoes
in the ground. The whole
country rotten.

\*

What was left buried in memorial gardens,
alongside statues to honour hunger:
children with milky fat
teeth in braces.
All we do now is eat.

# Haunted by Christ

## HILARY DAVIES

Richard Harries, *Haunted by Christ, Modern Writers and the Struggle for Faith*, (SPCK), £19.99

The difficulties with this book begin with its title. The OED defines 'to be haunted' as 'to be subject to the visits and molestation of disembodied spirits... imaginary beings, apparitions, spectres'; the verb also means 'to frequent a place or person'. Harries' choices of poets are 'ones for whom the pull of religion has been fundamental and in whose work we can best see what it is to believe or to protest against belief'. This raises lots of questions: if one rejects faith, does this mean one can still be 'haunted' by it? Does Christ bring the grace of the Holy Ghost or is he simply just a ghost, even a spook? Is the opposite of love hate or mere indifference?

The poets are: Emily Dickinson; Gerard Manley Hopkins; Edward Thomas; T.S. Eliot; W.H. Auden; Stevie Smith; R.S. Thomas; Edwin Muir; George Mackay Brown; and Elizabeth Jennings. It's the full gamut of Christian, indeed lapsed, even atheist, belief: cradle Catholics; Catholic and Anglo-Catholic converts; Anglican priests whose faith has been questioned; Presbyterians, Calvinists, and Calvinist Methodists who have fallen away and not returned to the fold. The list mirrors the fissiparous nature of Christianity since the Reformation, yet these important differences are often elided in Harries' presentations.

Firstly, let's be clear about what 'haunted by Christ' is not. Edward Thomas is a case in point. His presence here is, frankly, puzzling: although his poetry is haunted by longing, by a sense of the barrenness of his emotional and creative life that produced suicidal thoughts; this is in no wise the same as being 'haunted by Christ'. One of the last entries in his dairy was 'I never understood quite what was meant by God': incomprehension, rather than haunting, not even Harries' 'entirely negative attitude to religion', which might suggest the engagement produced by hate. Adducing St. Augustine to give weight to the idea that the human heart 'is restless until we rest in you' is not enough to make every unhappy agnostic or atheist a believer *à son insu*.

Faith, as all persons of faith know, is not the sugary consolation that a certain strand of secularism would have us believe. It is a struggle for meaning in the face of both the gift of creation and its horror; it is also a belief that the significance of Creation is more than material and its existence more than temporal. Faith knows no 'achieve'; it is a process, and that process has, in human terms, different outcomes. This state is akin to our relationships with those we love; some withstand argument, misunderstanding, sorrow, even anger, precisely because a bedrock of love and trust underpins them; some are irreparably damaged, though we constantly return to them; and some exist on the edge of silence and separation. Looked at thus, we can better understand to what degree the diverse poets selected here may be 'haunted by Christ'.

Harries seems most comfortable in his discussion of W.H. Auden: he shows compassion towards Auden's commitment to love whatever the situation and despite the pain it might cause. The poet's 'sense of gratitude for existence', which suffuses his mature poetry, is something to which Harries feels attuned. He recognizes the celebratory and incarnational nature of much of Auden's work, quoting him approvingly on the gravitas of the light touch, in poetry as in theology: Auden was no confuser of seriousness with pomposity. Harries' account of Auden's faith and its expression makes clear that the poet chose in the end what Christian theology calls the 'via positiva'. This, of course, is not to be confused with the kind of imbecilic optimism with which atheists such as Richard Dawkins or Christopher Hitchens have tasked believers. On the contrary, believers have a very well-developed sense of why and how the world is not as it should be; but they recognise that the ground of this understanding is not reducible to human ameliorist philosophies. Cataphatic theology (as the via positiva is also known) affirms; it sees God as having attributes; it emphasises how what we experience in the world around us and in our passage through life may offer some, albeit imperfect, understanding of what God might be. This will include knowledge of suffering and attempts to meet it.

Eliot's evolution is more complex. Harries swiftly outlines Eliot's familiar, tortured and tortuous journey towards his reception into the Anglican church in 1927. Emily Hale gets a mention (though this book was written before the opening of the Hale/Eliot correspondence in January 2020), before Harries discusses 'Ash Wednesday' in the light of Eliot's faith. Much has been written about the importance of this densely allusive poem in Eliot's development. So it is somewhat disconcerting to read the following two sentences in close proximity to each other, 'Eliot believed a poem should be obscure', and '[The poem] is not a conundrum to be solved'. What can this mean? The poem is described as 'haunting', 'hallucinatory', 'incantatory' but nothing else. The uninitiated reader is left none the wiser. Harries then glosses 'Marina' as being born from Eliot's feelings for Emily Hale as his muse, 'a face through which grace comes'. But this is rather to ignore the finely interwoven textures of boat-building, futurity, voyage, paternity, ocean, death, hope, an evoked shore and landscape that the poem contains, to say nothing of its intense and subtle acoustic soundscape analysed so sensitively, for example, by Robert Crawford in his 2009 Warton lecture, 'T.S. Eliot's Daughter'. And there is no getting away from the fact that the complete lack of any discussion of *The Four Quartets* in this chapter feels weird.

Not least because we miss the opportunity to compare Eliot's major lyric investigation of the absence, and presence, of God with the work of R.S. Thomas. His presence in this study is inevitable, though it's a big assertion that

'For the last part of the twentieth century his poetry spoke more clearly than any other for, and to, the condition of all who raise the question of God in any serious way'. Harries' remarks about Thomas in the introduction reveal what he means by this: '[Thomas] reflected the feeling of those who experience God only as an absence.' The implication is that Thomas' poetry appeals to a secular worldview that is wary of affirmative statements about faith. Now, it is true that Thomas is regarded as *the* poet of the apophatic in modern English poetry (though what about Hill, conspicuously absent from this volume?). But here Harries blurs the crucial difference between apophatic theology and mere atheism. The first position, which goes back to Pseudo-Dionysius (fl. 6th century C.E), holds that, ultimately, we cannot speak of what God is since this would be to delimit a transcendent being. The second position, post-Enlightenment, post-Darwinian, post-Einsteinian, holds that there is no such thing as a transcendent being. The two views are palpably not the same.

R.S. Thomas became an Anglican minister because his mother thought it was a safe career with decent prospects. Thomas evidently found faith hard, perplexing, often unrewarding and evanescent; it didn't help that he also found his fellow human beings difficult to love. So what we find in his poetry are statements of lack, silence, absence. God is not there, or appears not to be there, which amounts to the same thing for many readers in a secular age. But it is not. This experience of spiritual desert is hardly unique to Thomas: it is a recognized part of the religious life – one thinks of St. John of the Cross, more recently Mother Teresa. The medieval world knew it as accidie, a descent through indifference into despair, the giving up of hope in the efficacy of prayer or faith at all. Is this what Thomas tells us about in his poetry? Harries seems unsure, in large part because Thomas gives conflicting answers to these questions. On the one hand, some assertions are in the grand tradition of apophatic theology, 'But the silence in the mind/ is when we live best, within/ listening distance of the silence/we call God'; elsewhere he appears to suggest God is the Deus absconditus, 'the sound of a man... testing his faith/ On emptiness, nailing his questions/ One by one to an untenanted cross'. But this too is in that tradition. From this to stating that 'few poets have been so fierce in their disbelief in a God of love, or in the presence of any kind of God with us', is quite a leap.

If Thomas' relationship to his God is at best damaged and enraged, it is at least orthodox (just). Others, such as Stevie Smith and Emily Dickinson, have preferred to have their arguments with the Deity at home. Smith's disagreements with Christianity echo those of many in the 20th century who are dissatisfied with a religion that appears to condone, even inflict, suffering. Famously, she elaborated her objections in an address given to the Humanist Society in 1957, 'On the Necessity of Not Believing'. Such criticisms stem, in part, from a conflation of institutionalised religion with the relationship of God to creation; it does not mean that Smith was any the less agonised by this problem. She, with Dickinson, is perhaps the poet most truly 'haunted by Christ' here, in the sense that Christ, or how others have presented Christ, is both rejected and ever-present, loved and abhorred, the Holy Ghost and the spook. Here is Smith in 'God the Eater', 'There is a god in whom I do not believe/ yet to this god my love stretches/ This god whom I do not believe in is/ My whole life, my life and I am his'. Dickinson, too, may have refused to go into the Puritan house of worship of her fathers, but all her poetic life was spent in furious dialogue with the Godhead, now angry, now accepting, 'I know that He exists/ Somewhere – in Silence – / He has hid his rare life/ From our gross eyes./... But – should the play/ Prove piercing earnest – / Should the glee – glaze – / In Death's – stiff – stare// Would not the fun/ Look too expensive!/ Would not the jest – /Have crawled too far!'.

Finally, we have two Catholic poets, Hopkins and Jennings. In them the two traditions of thinking about God, the positive and the negative, are most developed. Hopkins says it all in a letter to Robert Bridges that Harries, happily, quotes, 'You do not mean by a mystery what a Catholic does. You mean an interesting uncertainty... but a Catholic by mystery means an incomprehensible certainty'. Here we have a perfect expression of the paradox at the heart of faith: it is sustained by a bedrock of love and trust, even into madness and darkness where 'I wretch lay wrestling with (my God!) my God'. Harries seems unaware of the irony in Elizabeth Jennings' life that helped produce her mental instability, that her very Catholicism made her susceptible to falling in love with priests, a fact that lay behind the agonies of faith she expresses in her work and which manifested itself in several breakdowns. Instead he concentrates rather on her 'mysticism', on her focus on 'gentleness', her interest in 'fable and myth', which do not do justice to her powerful intellect and serious engagement with theology. What are we to make of the statement that 'death was always something of a preoccupation of Elizabeth Jennings': of what poet worth the name could this not be said? It is at the root of any 'struggle with faith'.

Harries' focuses exclusively on the 'terrible sonnets' of Hopkins' Dublin years, thereby passing over the great celebratory poems written in Wales and Oxford, and the eruption of mind and spirit that is 'The Wreck of the Deutschland'. This sheers off half of what Hopkins was, a bit like (and I say this in full connaissance de cause) talking about John Donne's religious verse without mentioning his erotic poetry. Yet Hopkins is, par excellence, the poet of the grandeur and misère of life with God. Is this exclusion because Harries is embarrassed by Hopkins' paean to Christ', 'the fire that breaks from thee then, a billion/Times told lovelier, more dangerous, O my chevalier!' Or thinks his readers might be? Christ goes down into the tomb, but he also walks with his apostles to Emmaus. To haunt, we remember, means to frequent.

One niggle: the book contains some upsetting editorial errors. The key word, 'death' is omitted from Hopkins' poem, 'No, worst there is none', leaving the poet as the author of the banal sentiment that 'all life does end'; there are typos, and misreadings, in 'To seem the stranger', and 'Patience, hard thing!'. Finally, with all this talk of God's presence and absence, there is a breath-taking booboo in the mis-definition of cataphatic in the chapter on R.S. Thomas:' I contrasted his [Auden's] *via positiva* with Eliot's negative or cataphatic way in which... we simply wait upon God with wordless longing.' Pseudo-Dionysius would turn in his grave.

# Time Management and other poems
## MARTINA EVANS

## Time Management

The Dalston night is still warm,
the jasmine strong. I'm wondering,
as I lock up, if these rotting windows
could keep anyone out. Even the wisteria
gets in and snakes dizzily around
the kitchen wall in September.

A musical groan from the balcony tells me
the night is not over for Donny
ensconced on the comfy orange corduroy
chair – it was for us but it's his now,
his striped marmalade coat
blending with the saffron cord.

He croons again to me – so
I stay a while but he knows
I'm itching to go. He stands up on
the garden table and figure-of eights
with the fairy lights – anything to stop me
deserting like a Gethsemane apostle.

My back aches and I want to finish
Season Three of *The Leftovers* so I can
work very hard tomorrow. I pluck
some leaves of catnip for him
before I go, his unsatisfied longing
a weight as I climb the stairs

to the bedroom where Dora
the Norwegian Forest Cat
sits beside the TV, waiting
her turn. She wants the special massage
I learned from a YouTube video
made by a confident man with a shaved head,
*Learn Reiki in just five minutes!*

## Pethidine

Dr Johnson, the registrar in his scrubs
and stethoscope – middle aged and
harassed, one of those men who started late
or didn't have the luck or neck to push
for consultancy. These men were more likely
to treat us like human beings.
And Dr Johnson had pushed the stretcher
up from Casualty himself. The patient,
Mr Driscoll smelling like a stale barrel
of porter was propped up, belting out
The Banks in a brimming baritone, his leg
wrapped to the knee in greens.
Johnson looking over his chart, asked me
four times if I was sure I could do
this foot. I was still young enough
to be taken as too young to be able
to take an X-ray. I can take feet,
they're easy, I shouted over
Driscoll swinging at his verse –
where we sported and played through
each green leafy shade. It was a lesson
in observation. Every time I saw greens
after that, I saw Johnson unwrapping
that leg on Christmas Eve,
the foot hanging out like a door
on its broken hinge, Driscoll
with his red mouth open,
like every other drunk on Pana,
his tongue pedalling furiously,
my hands slipping on the cassette
as he rounded to his finale, screaming out,
For the love of Jesus – On The Banks
of My Own Lovely Lee.

## Man Falls off Greenhouse I

There are moments at the photocopying machine
when it comes back, the panic and prickly

heat when I have to repeat again and again.
Repeats were mortal sins. 100, 200, 300% increase

in the radiation dose. Sister Patricia, grave face above
her white habit – the list of artefacts like a checking

of the conscience, remove all jewellery, false teeth,
toupees. And three Vincents' students asking that

man with the artificial haystack on his head, Have
you got any jewellery, false teeth or toupees?

Our six eyes on his head, his jaw out – No-uh!
before we go back behind the control panel

to turn the large knobs and peer out, puzzled
at the thatch we daren't snatch off his head.

I've had to look into the man's eyes to get it all
arm-achingly angled right, lined-up straight – the strain

has us giggling and scared by the time we arrive
in the viewing area, having slammed the three classic

skull views in their cassettes into the Darkroom hatch
AP, Lateral and Townes and waiting –

for what could we expect? We don't know, only
we are so pink and jittery, we draw Miss O'Peel's

notice down on our nineteen-year-old nervous heads
She reaches in for the films, hangs them up

for everyone to see – a grid of lines and clips
all across the bone. Disgusting! Unprofessional!

The doctors look at us, disgusted too, as she
walks past us into the X-ray room and bangs as much

as one can bang a lead-lined door. We never
see what happened in there or how he parts

with his wig, the three classic skull views sail out
again on the chemical-lined river of the processor

all by themselves this time, Yorick alone
that leveller – pure luminous bone.

# Man Falls off a Greenhouse II

*after John Donne*

That evening, newly qualified, my first time as a second on-call. The first on-call, some impressive twenty-six-year-old Senior has been coping alone. The unspoken rule is that she leaves you at home if possible but here I am at nine p.m., full of beans on toast, shaking in the IVP room before the man with leukaemia and a glass eye. They've laid him on the Tomo Table. Tomography is the mother of Catscan, grandmother of MRI – with a big noisy swing of a heavy tube on a pole it can take a slice of a kidney but I am trying to X-ray a skull and I only know the Skull Table, now preoccupied with a chaos of hurlers because Senior is wrestling with The Glen hurling team and many male supporters wearing raincoats clutter the waiting room as my man removes the eye. With a tear in my own eye, I touch his shoulder, begin gently. Only when I press the exposure button, the pole starts swinging because it's on Tomo and I have to repeat only now there's no penetration. It's a pale squib. So I turn up the kilovoltage not knowing that the button has reverted to Tomo and it swings again – loud, scraping, flies past his head, over and back. He's suffered enough.

He's suffered enough. I go out to apologise but he's put his eye back in so I have to ask him to take it out again – leave it, until I've checked the films. Because the socket is dry, it makes a noise I can't bear. But we go again. Only this time I fear he's moved. When I come out of the dark room, I bend down to collect my film to see a blur. Yes, he has moved so we have to have yet another go only he's already put the cork of his eye back in its socket, the dry sucking noise as he pulls it out again is awful although now everything is right, kilovoltage, position. Yes, Tomo button up and he's stony still only when I open the bucky tray, it's empty – I forgot the film! – and he's busy putting his very dry eye back in its hydroptic pocket. When Senior looks in on me, I'm crying, my sap sunk among the chemicals where the processor is beeping for the fixer which stinks like me, a sinful tormentor of the sick and she sits on the barrel of developer laughing, wiping her Senior eyes, Oh leave his eye in his head, Jesus, it's hard enough. Leave everything in, they'll know what they all are when they read the films tomorrow morning. Right so. Tomo button up, open the cones WIDE, no need for pretty pictures tonight, film in the bucky. Big breath now, Mr Callaghan. Hold it!

**Note**

I say 'after John Donne' because I've taken words from his 'A Nocturnal on St Lucie's Day' – 'hydroptic', 'sap sunk', 'chaos', 'squib'... (I was also thinking of the Gloucester's eye and his 'corky arms' in Lear) but maybe I don't need to say after John Donne – I don't like to have a lot of references if possible.

# Hackney Trident

I think of Aidan when I stand on a chair, shaking
as I should have been, considering what I found out afterwards –
that the fuse box didn't work. The current was
*running two ways in a loop –*
I think that was what the fourth electrician said.

It didn't trip for twenty years and I'd been worried all
that time if I'd remember how to wind the wire if it did trip
which it couldn't.

*Aidan's all you can afford, Martina*, John was laughing.
He said the same about Spud Murph
and the amorous plumber.

Aidan was very shook inside his too-big grey trousers, his legs
bending like ashplants, his grey stubble, the metallic sweet
smell of last night's alcohol,
hands trembling on the fixtures

Will he take a cheque? *Jesus, if you offered Aidan a cheque
he'd cry,* all of them squeezed into the van, waiting
for me to fork out so they could go.

*He's all you can afford, Martina.*

After Aidan, the devout Catholic electrician's white eyebrows were leaping,

*Did you know that washing machine had no earth? It's a disgrace for any man to leave it that way
in a house with young girls.*

What about boys and middle-aged and old people?

*And that thing!*

His chin snapped at the Hackney Trident, our 1920s cut-out
with its Flash Gordon look, it had a habit of humming, a zzzzzzssssing
so I didn't go down to it much.

When the devout Catholic died, his hitherto quiet side-kick
son turned up flaming drunk at 8.a.m.
*All right. All right. I know what I'm doing!*


Mick from UK Power Direct took it away in the end
He said the Trident could be *very classy,* but he didn't
say my rusty paint-splashed one was
although I still have a piece of its porcelain.

His parents were from Mayo and Kerry but he didn't say that
until we were alone.

I was lucky to have a Trident, if I was on
the other side of the road, I'd have
one of the Islington ones.

*We don't tell people we call them*
*Islington Deathboxes. You can't work on them live –*
*everything has to be off.*

And we didn't even have an earth, the old one
had rusted away back to Mother Earth.
Mick drilled a new one down.

The last time I tried John, he wasn't laughing.
He'd gone to collect Aidan in his flat,
*The man was cold in his bed*. John, already
scared by his exploding oesophageal varices.

*I'd say he was there a while, Martina.*

# Two poems, one in verse, one in prose
## ANDREW MEARS

## Self-Portraits in Sneeze Glass

On a dinosaur hunt, tree roots wrenched up are the arcane script of a badger cult.
We had better turn away before we are drawn into their sett.

Sprouting leeks in yoga poses are the eyes of needles in the dirt, I tell him
Stacked clouds are happened rain longing to recur, more sour with each fall.

A magpie lifts from the bent stone wall, coughs-up and the spring-sky swallows. My child
In pyjamas and wellington boots, finds clandestine biscuits wrapped in blue foil.

He licks pink icing, flinches from a bee. Pine needles gyre downstream, get caught
And quiver like decibel metres to applause. He still grips me by one finger and we walk.

Clans veer the bagtree squat with dogfruit, self-portraits in sneeze glass, we'd better turn away.
He is so certain when he says to me, 'Look! The river, it is following us.' I wish.

## Précis of Dying as Live Traditions

He pours orange juice on his muesli and her stomach turns water. He works a mouthful
from his gums. The twenty-one-year overcoat, near brand new, is too large, sackish as
he hangs it on her. The heater tilts on its bracket and pink dust gives up from the screws.
She holds it, a husband, while the front door swings. Still dapper, *Are you fit then, love?*

On the bus, he does not believe the itch in her arm. The rumble draws her nails across
the ache. He sees them as search parties flattening grass in lines, impacting roman coins,
broken plate. She wipes her mouth with the back of her hand, the back of her hand with
her ticket. He kisses her and children laugh unkindly at the sight. *Are you fit then love?*

He steadies her arm, lifts his good arm to the Drive, holds down her hat as they cross.
He is set at her elbow, her elbow with his hand, his hand on her elbow, a faltering rock.
A woman smokes too close to the door. They come under its sense, an automatic hush.
Antiseptic is the smell of cuts, as a girl, as she soaked in the tub. *Are you fit then love?*

Opened ribs are a church full of sky, heartbeat round and precise. A skein of black and
pink jungle cut from the lungs to an engine's wet draw. Then, on the ward the miracle
of his name like the first she spoke. He imagines columns of mites, crucially occult,
rising in the heat of the room. He opens a window a nurse closes, *Are you fit then love?*

# Thomas A. Clark: Into actual space

## MATTHEW WELTON

In June 2017 I approached Carcanet with the idea of producing a volume of Selected Poems by Thomas A. Clark. The process of putting the book together has involved going through dozens of pamphlets, cards and other small paper objects mostly published by Clark's own Moschatel press. The aim has been to create something that, in the context of a bound book of around two hundred pages, will serve the poems as sympathetically as those original publications.

Perhaps the most striking thing about the poetry of Thomas A. Clark is its aesthetic. Clark's poetry is recognizable for its simplicity, quietness and attention, and these values are present both in what the poems are saying, and in the way it is said. Most of the poems in the volume of selected poems, *The Threadbare Coat,* were first published by Moschatel, the small press Clark and his wife, the artist Laurie Clark, set up in 1973. In the original editions, the aesthetic goes even further, and presentation becomes an aspect of the form.

Each Moschatel publication usually features a single poem. In some instances the poem is very short – some poems have only a few lines, and some have only one line. In the poems that break down into stanzas, each stanza usually has a page to itself, even if that means two lines to a page. Some of the shorter poems are presented on a single sheet of card, around the size of a postcard. Sometimes that sheet is folded, like a birthday card, which, importantly, allows it to stand up. Some of the publications come in envelopes, and in some the pages are bound in a cover of a contrasting colour, and the binding is often stitched by hand. Some Moschatel publications present drawings by Laurie Clark, often of a small bird or a wildflower, alongside the poem. There are poems in which some of the words are in printed in colours other than black. The paper and card from which all these publications are made is of good quality, the kind of materials found at an art supplies store. Moschatel editions do not have ISBN numbers.

Making presentation an aspect of the form in this way means that all aspects of the presentation – layout of the page, illustration, paper, sequencing – may be part of the meaning or feeling of the poem. The turning of the page, for instance, can be a more tangible revelation than a stanza break or a line break, so allowing a line or stanza a page of its own will slow the pace of a poem. There is arguably an ethical aspect too: if something is sufficiently important or special to be included in a poem, then giving it a little more space in this way may mean the reader will give it a little more attention.

A stanza from Clark's poem *of woods & water (forty-eight delays)* might stand as something of a manifesto for this approach:

> you will have to walk
> all round it to see it

you will have to stay
with it to know it

In publishing with his own press, Thomas A. Clark has been able to approach poetic form in a way that includes every aspect of the poems' presentation. This understanding also takes in poetic form in a more conventional sense. In Clark's poems, the regular aspects of poetic structure, such as line and stanza, and the ways in which the language is used play a significant part in creating meaning.

With much of Clark's early writing, the work of concrete poets such as Eugen Gomringer and Dom Sylvester Houédard was a strong influence. Concrete poetry was something that Clark felt offered a stillness in the poem that rivalled signs or advertising – and therefore a way into a non-literary culture – and a basic vocabulary and lack of expertise.

The poem '*by kilbrannan sound*' shows how Clark makes use of the conceptual aspect of concrete poetry in his own writing. The poem consists of eight lines, each of which includes a single phrase. The opening line is 'the glare of a black stone', and each of the lines that follow is identical except that, for example, in the second line 'glare' is swapped to 'gleam', and in the third, to 'glimmer'. The pattern of substituting a word which begins with the consonant cluster 'gl', and refers to the way light behaves continues to the end of the poem. The poem's form is playful and direct and functions as much as a kind of discovery about language as the expression of a feeling or idea.

That sense of the poem as object, as a small carefully made thing, has persisted in Clark's practice. Like a small artwork, a poem that can be taken in almost at a glance can be held in the mind and carried around. This perhaps fits with the way people often remember not whole poems but lines and phrases. There are resonances and echoes around words, so the small poem, like a stone dropped into water, can ripple out.

In many of Clark's other poems, line and stanza are used in ways that appear more conventional. Again though, there is an attention and a quietness in the way these elements are used that contributes to the effect. Within each poem the stanzas are generally regular in length, often of four lines. The lines are also regular, and in many poems are of no more than six or eight syllables. The way the lines function feels like an important part of Clark's poetry: each line ends where the phrase ends. Within a longer sentence, these line-endings often mark a turn in the attention, and never feel like the kind of break that fractures the sense of the poem.

The folk song or poem is one influence here, and Lorine Niedecker and early Ian Hamilton Finlay – both poets influenced by folk poetry – are others. The modesty, the anonymity and the country feel of folk poetry and music find an echo in Clark's poems. The writing is not some grand literary endeavour but, like a jig or a slow air, something that matters without lasting too long.

The music of language contributes to the form of the poems in other ways too. Many of Thomas A. Clark's poems do not use punctuation, yet the rhythm of the phrasing and the sense of what is being said mean its absence does not feel like a loss.

The opening stanza of '*at dusk & at dawn*' gives a good illustration of Thomas A. Clark's approach to form:

> before the day begins
> or when the business of the day
> is over there are intervals
> densities of blue or grey
> when you stand on the brink
> of a different possibility
> a stillness that opens
> out into clarity or
> a subtlety that folds
> back into stillness again
> you might almost touch it
> an occasion in the air
> as steady as a great tree
> branching into delicate life

It is one of a number of Clark's poems that use fourteen-line stanzas though, while it may take the form of a sonnet, there is none of the usual formality. Instead, the movement of the poem brings a series of small surprises which might refresh the way we think of things.

The lack of punctuation here is unlike the lack of punctuation in some avant-garde poems where the unsettling of readerly assumptions is the aim. In Clark's poems, a momentary hesitation might allow the reader a means of sharpening wits, and deepening their connection to the poem.

Another feature common to Clark's poetry is the use of the second-person pronoun. It is a subtle innovation that opens up a number of possibilities. The poems are not necessarily tied to Clark as a protagonist. While he may, of course, be talking to myself, he might also be addressing a companion. And this technique may be a way of putting the reader at the centre of the action. In that sense it is 'you', the reader, who walks up a hill or stands by a loch.

A pithy view might be that Clark's poems bring together the lyrical elements of folk song and the conceptual approach of concrete poetry in a way that erodes the distinction between those two genres. Even his shortest, most formally playful poems, like '*the earthly paradise*' or '*cress & mint*', are rich in imagery and rhythmic phrasing. And the poems that seem to speak most from experience and to be most firmly rooted in nature, such as '*from a grey notebook*', play with language in ways that create parallels and variations.

Over a lifetime of writing, Thomas A. Clark's work perhaps aligns more closely to the kind of practice common in the visual arts than to the approach of many poets. The connection may be most evident in his and Laurie Clark's work in running Cairn, the gallery they first set up in Nailsworth in Gloucestershire and later at their home in Pittenweem in Fife. The connection is there, too, in the integration of Laurie Clark's drawings with Thomas A. Clark's poems in many Moschatel publications. Rather than simply illustrating the poems, the drawings give character. Their precision and lyricism matches that of the writing. And over a number of publications, the coherence of the visual and the poetic become gives the body of work a sense of continuity.

The bringing together of poetry and visual art is also an element of the influence Ian Hamilton Finlay has had on Thomas A. Clark's work. This influence may be felt both in the poetry and in the way Finlay's Wild Hawthorn Press may be seen as providing the example that Moschatel has followed.

A sharp insight into that influence is given in the approach to the materiality of the poem, revealed by Thomas A. Clark in conversation with David Bellingham at a symposium on Clark's work held at the Scottish Poetry Library in Edinburgh in 2016:

> Ian Hamilton Finlay, who in the mid-sixties, about the time that I first met him, made this astonishing little discovery that if you took a piece of card, and folded it in half, it could stand up and support itself. And then if you take the words and put them on the front of the card, something equally astonishing happens, which is that poetry comes out of the imaginative space, out of literary space, and into actual space.[1]

This refusal of literary space has a parallel in the ways in which Moschatel publications have been offered for sale. Without spines or ISBN numbers, much of Clark's poetry has been unavailable through bookshops, and it has been either from Thomas A. Clark himself at poetry readings or from Laurie Clark at small publishers' fairs or artists' book events that readers have been able to get hold of the work.

The ways in which Moschatel books are produced and sold might be understood as being a good fit for the modesty and intimacy of the poems. In refusing the conventions of production and exchange in this way, the press may be thought of as offering a quietly radical alternative to the practices of mainstream publishing. Taken together, the ethic of the press and the aesthetic of the writing offer readers a unique approach to how the practice of poetry might be carried out.

### Note

1 Bellingham D., 'Thomas A. Clark in Conversation with David Bellingham', *Journal of British and Irish Innovative Poetry* 11(1). (2019) https://doi.org/10.16995/bip.756

# Two Poems

## NILTON SANTIAGO

### *translated by Jenny Eilidh Levack*

## The Hermeneutics of a Snail

I bet a sunflower seed
that nobody knew that sheep don't drink running water
or that, on average, a person has more than 1460 dreams each year.
It's true, some owls seduce trees to get a smile out of the dead who dangle there or, simply, to swallow the
    tears that Baruch Spinoza shed
when he found out that all his philosophising on "the infinite divine substance"
(which for him was reality or God) was a load of tosh.
It's true, life seems all too much like a Brecht production
and loneliness nips us at our fingertips
even if we're passing through as zen-like monks or basil smoking screwballs.
Tell me, you, who is getting cold in my heart
and who refuses to leave the house without a high voltage kiss extinguisher
(an extinguisher may be as innocent as a wooden knife that goes back to the forest to attack the sawmills).
Following the same logic, I now think that the ocean you have under your bed
has all the manners as a cat, meaning, that whenever it feels like it,
it spits out bottles containing love messages as though they were a fur ball.
It would be a crime to say that for some Pre-Socratic philosophers
twenty-something girls are full of good intentions
or that philosophical butterflies are the solution to forgetting Wagner.
Certainly, like those men, there are also astronauts who don't know how to ride a bike and who easily confuse
    falling in love with wanting to eat one of the dimples in your cheek.
But what the hell, all of our first girlfriends left us with our hearts smashed to smithereens and in my country
    we thought the armed conflicts wouldn't get out of hand.

You know all too well that you don't have to kidnap an office worker's consciousness to realise that the world
    has got a screw loose:
it is sociologically acceptable to loot a bank or to trick a cherub into letting you into heaven in exchange for
    bird food,
but report a politician who has won the lottery 20 times in a year
and you'll probably have to pack up your tears and flush them down the toilet.
Even so, don't play the bemused card,
write with a feather plucked from your back,
go out onto the street without opening your wings
and you'll see that neither you are quite what you thought

# I Went to Dinner and Ainhoa and Bruno and They Say It Could Be Because of the Language that We Don't Understand Each Other

Freud said there were two ways to be happy in this life:
one is to play the fool and the other is to be the fool. I have certainly
been happy both ways and amongst your scrambled freckles also.
Bruno would call this opening to a poem a pathetic speech
of soluble love, good enough to be published in a porcupine hairdresser catalogue.
I agree with him, so instead I'll talk to you about the children
that play football with the scraps of detonated bombs
fallen on the Al Bahrein school in Gaza or, even better,
let's talk about this waitress who has a smile bursting with butterflies
and into whose ear I've just whispered that if you take away a cat's whiskers
it can lose its balance and fall over.
Autumn has just arrived fleeing from the news that fill fish tears with salt,
Bruno doesn't agree that we should keep on talking about fish,
or the fines issued by the stars for us double parking
opposite the heart of a girl like you, but it doesn't matter,
if for some reason the sun stopped casting its light,
it would take us 8 minutes here on earth to realize,
so I will take advantage of these 7 minutes to tell you that hitting
your head against the wall consumes 150 calories per hour, my friend,
or tell you that Gina and I have spoken on the phone again for no reason.
*The language, the language, it could be a problem* says Ainhoa,
but if even dolphins and whales can understand each other
when they take the piss out of divers, if even that fish that lives at the bottom of the sea
and has teeth so big it can't close its mouth can understand
why the tides and university fees go up each year when it reads the newspaper
but then I remember that morning I asked you if '*¿Te gusto mucho?*'
and you, smiling, asked me whether that meant '*If I like you?*' or '*if you like me?*'
while the northern lights were drawing up between that look of yours
and the sunrise. Bruno says that one gram of gold can expand up to 20km
and that I leave you legal tender under your door
between your bed and my sheets, he also tells me to stop all this nonsense
and to put all the carcass of this poem on the barbecue.
Then I order another coffee because I can't handle this drowsiness
that I get from facing the stars at the bottom of this glass
and suddenly you say that 100 cups of coffee drunk in the space of four hours
can technically cause death, and I think I have already taken 99
and there are 60 seconds left for me to start saying something in this poem,
so I look out the window to see that man selling lighters
as though his heart were one great butane lamp
and you stare at him too until you realize that you know how to talk to birds
and suddenly you are the bird, Bruno, and the honey feathers
falling from another bird is the only language that I understand
when I think of the unmentionable Gina.
This poem is like the bottom of the sea wounded in the stomach by the fish
that pitch up – alone – to die at the bottom of your heart
But I'm wrong, life is far too abstract to speak about her
in a poem when you can't sleep and suddenly you wake up,
and turn off the alarm clock or fling it out the window
and you pick up the pieces of what's left of yourself to reach the kitchen
and make yourself another coffee
and suddenly it dawns on you that love is another lie from the stars,
and the coffee and the water and the fridge covered in annotations
and mistakes and defrosted caresses and feathers from all the pillows
where you have deposited your dreams
and even your honey on toast are lies

and the orange is just an orange when you cut it in half, like your heart.
You have breakfast standing up with the sound of the news headlines in the background:
random bomb attacks against entire populations of anteaters,
vaccines not developed from the pressures of pharmacists,
several hidden bank accounts inside a sea snail,
by the way, did you know a hamster's eyes can fall out
if you hang it upside down?
And suddenly you switch off the TV and go to the metro and start reading
and you realize you that for years you've been reading the same poem
written by the rain and that cat tears are poetic material too;
the solitude of the same girl that you see each morning
with fragile ribs and red lips, like the high clouds
where God's dreams are cooking,
and suddenly you arrive at work, as disorientated as a horse in chess
and in a yawn you go back home with a startled look
and you realize you have forgotten the language of the birds.
Then I think that I'm like those fish that don't get bored in a fish tank,
because their memory only lasts for two minutes
and it's like they are born again and again,
again and again until they forget their heart,
and it's then when I'm dying to take the 100th cup of coffee in four hours.

### Note

Nilton Santiago was born in Lima though has lived in Barcelona for many years. He has published five poetry collections, *El libro de los espejos* [*The Book of Mirrors*] (II Copé Prize of the XI Poetry Biennial, Lima 2003), *La oscuridad de los gatos era nuestra oscuridad* [*The cats' darkness was our darkness*] (which received the International Young Poetry Prize from the José Hierro Poetry Center Foundation, Madrid 2012), *El equipaje del ángel* [*The Angel's Luggage*] (XXVII Tiflos Poetry Prize, Visor Libros 2014), *Las musas se han ido de copas* [*The Muses Have Gone Out Drinking*], (which was awarded the prestigious Poetry Prize *Casa de América de Poesía Americana*, Visor Libros 2015) and, recently, *Historia universal del etcetera* [*A Universal History of Etcetera*] awarded with the Vicente Huidobro International Poetry Prize, Valparaíso Editores 2019).

Also author of the book of chronicles *Para retrasar los relojes de arena* [*To Delay The Hourglasses*] (Vallejo & Co., 2015), a number of his poems have been collected in the anthologies *A otro perro con este hueso* [*To Another Dog With This Bone*, Costa Rica 2016] and *24 horas en la vida de una libélula* [*24 Hours In The Life Of A Dragonfly*, Bulgaria 2017].

# Grosseteste in Two Chapters
## *1–Shedding light on common objects*
### IAN BRINTON

The first words of Robert Grosseteste's treatise *De Luce* (*On Light*) seem to offer a very reasonable opening into a brief look at one of the most innovative small poetry presses of the 1960s and 70s:

> The first corporeal form which some call corporeity is in my opinion light. For light of its very nature diffuses itself in every direction in such a way that a point of light will produce instantaneously a sphere of light of any size whatsoever, unless some opaque object stands in the way.

The opacity which appears to have brought a close to one of the most imaginative and forward-looking presses of the second half of the twentieth century was both financial and murderous: the costs of producing books of such a high standard and, in 1978, the murder in Leeds of one of its co-founders, John Riley.

A graduate from Pembroke College Cambridge, John Riley had been a school contemporary of Gordon Jackson and in his pamphlet account of the setting up of the Grosseteste Press (Asgill Press, 2016) the latter recalls how in their teens they had been drawn together by a mutual interest in poetry: by the reading of it, thinking about it and the sharing of ideas concerning their aspirations to write it. As Jackson was to put it this shared interest led to him being introduced to the Black Mountain poets of the 1950s and to the work of Ian Hamilton Finlay's Wild Hawthorn Press. Jackson made a journey to Finlay's home at Stonypath which lay on the side of a quiet valley in the Pentland Hills and he was struck by the poem-sculptures the poet was working on. In Stephen Bann's illustrated essay that accompanied the catalogue of Finlay's work exhibited in 1972 at the Scottish National Gallery of Modern Art he referred to the transformation of landscape that the artist had been responsible for at Stonypath:

> But the main transformation cannot be explained simply in terms of physical change. What Finlay has pre-eminently done is to irradiate this area with meaning, through the exactly gauged installation of inscriptions, constructions and other types of poetic work.

Bann went on to suggest that the structure of the place had a 'metonymic connection with the world adjoining' and rather than being a part of the hillside was instead 'the world's image'. Jackson's pilgrimage had also been to see Finlay's Wild Hawthorn Press and he came away with the determination to set up his own working press in Lincoln. Since Finlay's work had been recognised among the most beautiful and the most permanent things being done in the field of experimental poetry, Gordon Jackson could not have chosen a better master. The most immediate result of that visit was the setting up of the Grosseteste Press in Stonefield Avenue in Lincoln and the publication of what became central to the new British Poetry scene that had been heralded in early 1966 with the setting-up of Andrew Crozier's and Jeremy Prynne's *The English Intelligencer* in its typed foolscap format.

However, it is worth recalling Charles Olson's short poem from 1950 which put a clear emphasis upon our awareness of where we spring from:

> These Days
>
> whatever you have to say, leave
> the roots on, let them
> dangle
>
> And the dirt
>
>> Just to make clear
>> Where they come from

In the light of this thought it should not be overlooked that the story of the setting up of Grosseteste Press harks back to the earlier world of Gael Turnbull's Migrant Press which had started in Worcester under the name Migrant Books in 1957. That new venture had attempted to introduce into England the work of certain American writers who had interested Turnbull through his reading of *Origin*, *Black Mountain Review* and Jonathan Williams's Jargon Books. Migrant Press was to produce Edward Dorn's short prose piece *What I See in the Maximus Poems* in 1960 and, one year later, Roy Fisher's *City*. Turnbull had also edited a magazine titled *Migrant* and in the last two issues the connection between the world of what was happening in American poetry and what was finding a new voice in England could be seen in the placing side-by-side Charles Olson and Hamilton Finlay whilst also printing William Carlos Williams's fine reminder of the need of poets and publishers to refuse to settle into conformity:

> The goal of writing is to keep a beleaguered line of understanding which has movement from breaking down and becoming a hole into which we sink decoratively to rest.

Given the background of Gordon Jackson's interest in Hamilton Finlay's work and in what was happening in America it comes as no surprise to find that the first few volumes to issue from the Grosseteste Press should include early work by John James and Michael Grant, Jim Burns and Jeremy Prynne. One must not of course overlook the early work of John Riley and Tim Longville, both of whom had been taught at Cambridge by Donald Davie, and both of whom had also appeared in *The English Intelligencer*.

Gordon Jackson writes about how he had purchased what became the Grosseteste machine from a firm in Essex which also provided him with a set of used 11pt Garamond. He then had the rollers recovered with treothene before getting new inks from a firm in Leeds and a hand-lever guillotine. He also recalls the journey back from Leeds to Lincoln with these accessories in the back of the van and Tim Longville 'hanging on to the metal table while the legs and blades threatened him at every savage bend'. It was 1966 and the sheets of the first volume, *Common Objects*, were printed and interleaved, the pages were cut and collated before being stapled, trimmed and finally numbered. As the last minutes of the year were being counted Gordon Jackson and his wife Hélène along with Tim Longville sat at the kitchen table in Stonefield Avenue with the first of what was to become one of the most interesting small presses of the time.

John Riley had suggested that the new press be called 'Bread and Wine' after the Hölderlin elegy of that title which he and Longville had been working on and which Riley had sent to Michael Hamburger in 1963. A second name was also mooted as the Occasional Press before a decision was finally taken in acknowledgement of Gordon Jackson's reading of a biography of the medieval Bishop of Lincoln, Robert Grosseteste. With that having been agreed upon the business was formally registered with Gordon and Hélène Jackson as directors and Tim Longville and John Riley taking up the position of editors.

Those translations of Hölderlin were to become the fifth publication from the new press and *In the Arms of the Gods* appeared in 1967. Longville was to recall later that since Riley was working in Oxfordshire and he was based in Staffordshire they would travel to Lincoln together having met up first in Birmingham and that the editorial meetings which took place at Stonefield Avenue were often weekend-long ones spent folding, stitching and packing the latest book. Longville also recalled that the final revision work on the shared venture of Hölderlin translations was in fact done in the bar of the Midland Hotel in Birmingham while waiting for the 'little, local, stopping-at-every-lamp-post train'.

*Common Objects*, printed in an edition of 215 copies, was a collection of short poems by Riley and Longville that had been written between 1962 and 1964 and they included two pieces that were dedicated to Jeremy Prynne and Joel Oppenheimer. The former bore the title 'The Advent' and included the lines 'preoccupied // by light' an early foreshadowing perhaps of the importance of the work of Robert Grosseteste. Oppenheimer had been a student at Black Mountain College learning about writing from Charles Olson and he had been published in Robert Creeley's *Black Mountain Review*. At one point in *Common Objects* four lines, placed alone on a white page, suggest something of that intensity of interest which all three creators of the Grosseteste Press were to share in their creation of newness:

He kept himself
    obsessed
which is different from
    self-interest.

As Gordon Jackson recalls one of the most important reasons for the setting up of this new press was to print and publish the poetry of John Riley and in 1967 the second volume to be issued was his collection *Ancient and Modern*. In 1975 Tim Longville produced the *Grosseteste Descriptive Catalogue* and his comments on the first publication of a collection of John Riley's poetry make clear the significance of the event:

The peculiar excitement of this book for me was when I first read it as it is now, the gradual opening and giving of a language, from page to page, new life, astonishment, heart and art. Suddenly the press had a poet, the fun had a purpose.

The book's title had been taken from a poem which had first appeared in *The English Intelligencer* and Gordon Jackson recalls recognising the fine ear, the Dantesque lines and the patient development of thought:

Away from the house the snow falls slanting,
And trees almost in leaf in yesterday's sun
Put on today an elegant new shape,
A complex, streamlined growth...

*Ancient and Modern* was published in an edition of 321 copies with a cover photograph of a tree which had been taken by Riley himself.

1967 also saw the publication of five more books from the new Grosseteste Press including the remarkable broadsheets of John James's *The Welsh Poems* which were presented in a stiff blue wallet in an edition of 400 copies. The wallet contained two versions from the mediaeval Hendregadredd MSS along with an original poem and it was designed in two hours on a train back from Newcastle after the Sparty Lea Festival that had been organised by the young Barry MacSweeney. As Jackson was to put it

The exultation is a Welsh form that asks for space and plenty of sound. We chose (and here we all claim responsibility) an orihon fold in a stiff envelope. The poems spread out over the broadside page, while on the reverse side was a half-tone copy of the Welsh manuscript, printed in randomly mixed read and black inks so that each copy was more or less unique. The folio scale of the pages and antique laid paper in three different colours make for an effect of the sort of elegance proper to the older books. A lovely thing and now a rare one.

One of the impressive aspects of these early years of the Grosseteste Press was Gordon Jackson's determination to consider each publication as a singular event and a 'book would be shaped as it needed' rather than 'according to a general pattern imposed on all productions.' And so when it came to publishing those translations of Hölderlin that Riley and Longville had been working on the longer lines demanded a landscape format rather than the portrait style which was the more normal one in book production. This concern for the way a book looked was a reflection of a deep respect for the contents contained within the covers and when John Hall's collection *Between the Cities* appeared in 1968 the shape of the publication was dictated by the design on the cover, a Renaissance view of pilgrims making their way to Jerusalem, and the poems were printed on blue Basingwerk Parchment.

As 1967 moved into 1968 a major shift was to take place in the production of Grosseteste volumes. With Tim Longville's first collection of poems, *Familiarities*, and Michael Grant's first collection, *The Fair*, there was a development away from the publications which had required only centre stapling which limited the number of pages to about thirty-six. *Familiarities* as a collection of poems that required sixty pages and with Grant's volume needing even more at eighty a new way of production was required and Gordon Jackson recalls how 'We had to find stitching, a saddle press for the spine, a gluepot and ammunition, a nipping press, and boards for the case binding.' With the Longville volume Jackson also chose to use antique laid and to print the titles of each poem in red hence doubling the labour required for the printing. The Grosseteste Press was developing.

In 1968 when Tim Longville founded *Grosseteste Review* the early issues were printed on the Grosseteste Press and issued from Stonefield Avenue. The initial aim was to produce three issues each year and Jackson still recalls it as 'a splendid venture' with a list of contributors that was truly remarkable. The first set of three issues presented work by Roy Fisher and J.H. Prynne as well as early poems by Barry MacSweeney and John Hall. Appropriately enough Gael Turnbull featured in the first two issues and by issue three the younger poets such as Peter Riley and David Chaloner had found a place. As Prynne and Turnbull were placed alongside the Americans Gilbert Sorrentino and Carl Rakosi and Elaine Feinstein appeared next to Lew Welch it must have been very apparent to those interested in the new British Poetry that the linking of what was taking place in England and what was happening in the post-Black Mountain world of America was being forged in a way that was to have a lasting effect upon what was to happen over the following years. By the end of 1968 the *Review* was well established with a reasonable list of subscribers and the aesthetic character developed by the other Grosseteste publications.

*The White Stones*, that early volume by J.H. Prynne which was republished by New York Review Books in 2016, was the largest work undertaken by the press. At just short of one hundred pages it possessed what Peter Gizzi, the editor of the NYRB edition, called a 'generous surface structure and energetic belief system'. Jackson's own recollections of the book's production tally precisely with that comment:

> On a tall page with generous margins the crisp blocks of type on antique laid paper still placate the critical eye of the book designer. As does the cover design by Ron Harrison in black and white on dark green linson.

For the Grosseteste Press it became Jackson's 'high water mark as a designer'. Printed in an edition of 477 copies it became for Longville 'something of a totem, white whale, magic mass' and in his *Descriptive Catalogue* he was to direct those interested in the volume to the comments made by Donald Davie in *Thomas Hardy and British Poetry*. However, the financial difficulties in producing books of such high quality were inevitably to have an effect and Longville's comment also suggested a major gap between interest and purchase:

> The number of those who've read it, admired it, attacked it, worried over it, is out of all proportion to the number of copies we seem to have sold.

And in an unpublished letter from Gordon Jackson to Jeremy Prynne the founder of the Grosseteste Press bemoaned the fact that the Student Bookshop seems to be the 'only one that will stock our things'.

Much of the rest of the year 1969 was taken up for Jackson with the publication of the next three issues of *Grosseteste Review* and in the autumn issue one could read Prynne's short review of Chris Torrance's *Green Orange Purple Red* collection of poems that had just appeared from another new press started by Andrew Crozier and taking its name from the Woolwich ferry. Prynne referred to Torrance's 'brilliant stream' which was 'still working in those rare places where not flooded by effluent' and urged readers of poetry to look for themselves at this new style of work:

> Very well, you say, obliging but puzzled reader; but what in fact and motion do these poems actually sound like? Read them and find out; what more do you want?

The last two books printed on the Grosseteste machine were John Riley's collection of poems from 1967–1969, *What Reason Was* and Bobby Byrd's *Places & Memphis Poems*. For Jackson the Riley was the most valuable book he produced:

> The bold cover uses large condensed woodletter in the title, and a fillet of Russian folk art in brown on yellow, and lettering in normal black.

As he saw it, the effect was striking and as an indication of the importance of these poems it is interesting to note how Carol Rumens chose one of them, 'The Attraction', as her 'poem of the week' presentation in *The Guardian* in 2017:

> There are poets one instinctively trusts as well as those one instinctively distrusts, even while instinctively distrusting both those instincts. John Riley, for me, is firmly in the first category. I think he says what he means, though the movement of his mind is quick, and opposite positions may be juxtaposed.

As 1970 moved towards 1971 Tim Longville took over the running of publications doing the text typing and dealing with the Lincoln printers who were now replacing the Stonefield Avenue press that had been hard at work since those *Common Objects* had appeared some five years earlier and it is perhaps worth noting that one of the poems in that first volume had been titled 'The Editor of Light' opening with a reference to Paul Léautaud who had at the age of twenty-eight in 1900 had published a volume of extracts from writers of the contemporary scene which included Barbusse, Bataille and Corbière sitting alongside Laforgue and Mallarmé:

> Paul Léautaud refractory
> and factory
>
> of light
> de lumière...

Those words which had opened up Robert Grosseteste's tract *De Luce* shed a light over the developing world of British poetry in the late 1960s and the *Grosseteste Review* with its associated book publications was to continue under the leadership of Longville and Riley for some years to come. But that is another story.

# Hem and Other Poems

## GENEVIEVE STEVENS

## Hem

How long has it been like this?
For a moment I didn't know
if she meant the skirt or my life.
But as she then cleared space to lay flat
the hem, her hands existing only
for that bit of fallen fold,
well –
I put the answer away.

We grew silent.
Me appalled by the everything almost said
out loud
or perhaps it's all been heard
in other rooms, older houses

And the longer I sat watching her,
the more I became grateful for the hem –
for its sudden, simple undoing,
for her – always
knowing which stitch is best,
grateful too for that pristine exchange –
my need, her capacity.

## Scotch tape, ruler, pencil

*After Agnes Martin*

What astonishing peace when the whole thing is
recurrence. To trust only

the grid – a geometry of silence
for colour to arrive into and rest, a surface

so deep it folds back on itself and says
nothing.  Again. And again.

But how to square a life lined with conviction
and paintings unwilling to talk?

And was it enough, to leave yourself out?

## A Vast Upheaval of Matter

Marshland, still.
By the river – someone's tent, clothes, sleeping bag.
The shock of all that life happening undisturbed,
what else don't you know?

*

As we walked from the grave, he gave me his coat to carry
and on the Warwick road knelt to unlace his shoes,
apologising softly he passed them up to me
and when we reached home neither of us mentioned
the bin men re-filling bins,
or the child sellotaping an oak leaf to the sycamore
or the smallness of his father's corpse.

## Reds

One night she fell so hard her voice changed.
She took up smoking again

(Reds this time) and god she was forever
wiping surfaces, leaving rooms.

Perhaps because she never said, she thought
I could not see. But there it was –

pulling at the neckline of her nightie
till the day came she gave up standing

and just sat on the kitchen floor, sat there
for so long she became an abstract –

her eyes, it was her eyes that went first,
clogged with colour beyond my years.

# Still too much sky

## ALEX HOUEN

*A diversion between Curzio Malaparte's 'Ancora Troppo Cielo'*
*and Virgil's 'Eclogue IV'*

I.
Who'd have thought the horizon is just the edge
of a face mask? Who'd have thought that a coppice
wood could do the police in different birds?
Time to essay up fresh voice again for this
age now is so far from golden and closer
to pangolin – most widely trafficked creature
and viral host to humans. A pangolin's
tongue is rooted in its pelvis and so long
it keeps it rolled up in a mouth-pouch that is
like an internal mask. The Sibyls avoid
pangolins, and Marianne Moore was right about
them: we can only approach them with syllables.
       My daughter says no, the age we are in is
actually six, and why be the film's heroine
when you can be its horse emerging from surf?
Each morning after sleep's harvest I give her
honey and she watches some tipping point in
the form of an old walrus, say, tumbling down
a cliff face, or a troop of chimps feasting on
Colobus monkey, or a dog-man cartoon.
O Muse, there's so much assorted voice that speaks
without a mouth these days – and I don't just mean
writing or thinking. After hearing breaking
news of fresh deaths yesterday she gave her own
name to her imaginary friend...


II.
Each time I drive us closer to the town's first
circle I see its factory injecting
vast vats of sleep into the sky to make some
kind of sugar. It's so white, the sky, with us
always behind glass, living in capsule form.
Perhaps the sky models social distancing
because sky, like style, is at least two persons.
I don't know. I keep dreaming I'm eating glass
while speaking bits of the day to a person
I can't see
              the person
                        I'm breaking up with
              Fortune's rule
                        it's just what happens
                  it's *what just happened?*
              wearing public measures
                        as pangolin scales
                        news ticker
                          'gold's dilemma'
                  and the terrible sadness of hands
         almost angelic
       for being incomplete

III.
When you were just two you did a green scribble,
pointed to it and said 'House!', and I said 'Yes,
that's true'. Now I come alive when I'm watching
you design homes with all their surroundings, like
this one you've made from blocks of molten lava,
bone, glass, and glowstone, with cactus tiles and snow
carpeting, while outside you pour out fresh plot
and hatch on it the eggs of horses, pandas,
wolves, pigs, rabbits, cats, polar bears, and chickens.
There's even a cross made with blocks of running
water 'for the person who died inside there',
and when you accidentally break llamas
into this home, yes, you can always live in
trees and get rid of the roaming skeletons
by touching them with your fingers just as you
might your face. Then, sure, it does make sense to kill
a bit more time by swapping your golden boots
and armour for a pair of diamond leggings...

IV.
No, that's not tinnitus and not a siren,
nor a herd of distant running pangolins,
it's the sound of a loss of scale. A measure
of two metres is the sublime now, but hard
to fathom with all the sky packed into it.
While some scale Everest by their interior
stairs, some say the sublime is 'oven-ready'
or becoming an antibody. Heaven
knows what beauty is. We keep being encouraged
to use Italy as a mirror. Somewhere,
a man is fishing inside his goldfish tank.
Are these symptoms of Italy and should I
call a doctor? When a pangolin rolls up
into a ball perhaps its showing itself
all tongue, wholly on the scale of tongue. Curled up
asleep last night I dreamt I was speeding through
London empty as a shelf
                              I was flying by
            like an algorithm
                        in the dark
                  rollerblade happy, carefree.
            When I awoke I washed
                              my hands of it.
Can't help myself.
            That's the closest I've come
      to a human being
for days...

V.
O my love, I love that you can keep mocking
death in the name of Italy, the numbers
of Italy. Traces of old disaster
may remain, lurking, but I believe in our
collage as vision of a future – the one
we made from magazines. Its temple ruins are
yours to plug in, and when you do the huge face
that appears between the columns belongs not
to Apollo nor Saint Valentine nor Pan
but to the character you'll grow with your friends
out of the ruins. Without that heaven would be
unbearable.
                  *Who can escape their nature?*
asked the Sibyls. Yet none can tell what nature's
hiding now, nor what any nature can do.
So keep hatching those eggs of pandas, horses,
wolves, rabbits, cats, bats, chickens, and polar bears.
Keep planting lilac, rose, and peony around
your cross of water. And have courage, my love;
the eyes of the temple face are brown and large
as the boxing gloves you wear to look up to
the sky

*March–April 2020*

# Reviews

## Numinous Signs

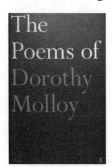

Dorothy Molloy, *The Poems of Dorothy Molloy* (Faber & Faber) £16.99
Reviewed by N. S. Thompson

Dorothy Molloy's poetry is rooted in a pre-Reformation world numinous with religious signs and symbols. Born in 1942, she moved as a student from the strict Catholicism depicted in Edna O'Brien's novels to the more joyful traditions of Spain. But this was Franco's Spain before the decades of mass tourism, Costa del Sol, Costa del Crime and supermarkets full of chorizo, take-away paella and endless ruddy bottles of Rioja, which can be a most redeeming feature. And it informs the spirit of her poetry, not so much as a loss of innocence as a gaining of knowledge, where she affirms her faith not with quiescent piety but rather a heart-filling radiant joy in the created world, despite all the stones placed in the pilgrim's path.

Under Franco's rule, and still pole-axed by the Civil War, the country had remained a mainly rural backwater alienated from its internationally celebrated but exiled painters, poets and filmmakers: Picasso, Dalì, Alberti, Buñuel (to say nothing of the poet Federico Garcia Lorca, assassinated in 1938). In many ways it was virgin territory, ruled by images of the Virgin, a backcloth that could be moulded into whatever youthful fantasy one wished and, if still virginal, Dorothy Molloy had a lively imagination to cloak it with her imagery. But it was also still the world of Hemingway, that *aficionado* of death in the afternoon in *la corrida*. In 'Trophy' the end of the bull is described as 'the dagger/plunged to the hilt in its scabbard/of flesh'; the audience erupts in hedonistic approval, men throwing hats in the air, women kicking up polka-dot skirts, flinging underwear, flowers and phone numbers at the matador, who performs the final rite on the bull. The cinematic panorama of the raving public and its spectacle then becomes focussed on the poet's persona as the matador searches for a suitable recipient for the trophy of the bull's ears and testicles and the poem concludes as the matador 'sees my whitening face,/and throws the whole bloody lot in my lap'. The shock of this reversal is not simply in the

action, but is foreshadowed briefly by the persona's 'whitening face' and the reader wonders what is to come next: will she denounce the violence in rage or is the pallor a prelude to vomiting at this last outrage on the bull? What comes next (and last in the poem) is typical of the Molloy's nuanced control of language: the everyday phrase of 'the whole bloody lot' is both expressive of disgust and yet its very colloquial tone, as if she were relating the punch line in the humorous mode of a would-you-believe-it tale to friends in the pub, perfectly expresses the alienation from that scene and its bloody action. It is a macabre comedy that reminds one of Geoffrey Hill's similar use of the colloquial mingled with high drama at the end of the third poem in his Wars of the Roses sequence 'Funeral Music' where the dying vanquished gasp an ambiguous 'Jesus'.

Endings are a particular forte for Molloy, both in her poems and during the course of her life, before it came to its final tragic end. Perhaps the greatest break was with her Irish Catholic upbringing, but then tempered by the life she found in Catholic Spain. Many poems reflect the difficult changes in life, scenery and love. 'Sweet Nothings' reifies the expression into a series of metaphors of confectionary for the exchange of sweet kisses, seeing them as 'marshmallows', 'caramels' and 'Dark liqueurs' which then mutate into the phonology of 'bilabial plosives', 'glottal stops' and 'fricatives'. Finally, having filled her with 'Turkish Delight', the lover leaves her with 'a jelly baby'. Again ending on this colloquial phrase is jarring and full of pathos.

And for all the adventurousness of stepping away from the known of home, many poems reflect the resulting suffering and ignominy of intrusions on the self and the body, especially, and particularly, when that body is female and finds itself at the mercy of a male. Opening oneself up to new experiences can appear attractive as an excitement but it has its dangers and can cruelly wound. Often the two elements are part of a single narrative sequence. The poems here range from 'Floating with Mr Swan' where the poet is a tranquillised Leda mouthing 'I wuv ya. I wuv ya' through her sedated lips to more oblique descriptions of abuse. 'First Blood' recalls the reaction of a lover jealous of her amorous past. Over dinner with him the poet deliciously recaptures the fashions of first adulthood with her first boyfriend: shocking pink lipstick, fish-net stockings and high-heeled shoes. The current lover is not amused and the poem ends:

Someone is screaming 'For each one
you fucked'. Someone is calling me 'Whore'.

The sudden shift to an unidentified 'someone' ably conveys the surprise and the can-this-be-happening-to me of the violence by a known someone to a violent someone else. Happily other attentions from the male are less traumatic, if a nuisance. By contrast, the sensation of being in a woman's body is explored in more positive terms in such poems as 'Playing the Bones', 'Envelope of Skin' and 'Bones'. In the first and third of these poems, the poet's bones are seen as the scaffolding that supports life; indeed a comforting part of the body as we see in the first and third lines repeated in the villanelle and which conclude it as a couplet:

I feel the bones that will lie in my grave;

They live inside me, snug, in their enclave.

This poem from the second of her three collections *Gethsemane Day* (2006) introduces the poems that deal with the imminence of that grave. At the end of 2003 the poet was diagnosed with cancer of the liver and many poems reflect her stoic and courageous reaction to the news and subsequent therapy, most notably in the title poem to the collection. Having had a sample of her liver taken for analysis, from her hospital bed she asks:

What ferments in pathology's sink? Tonight they will tell me, will
proffer the cup,
and, like it or not, I must drink.

But, in other poems, the poet endures both tests and treatment in macabrely comic terms, as in 'Freed Spirit' and in 'Radiotherapy' where 'The side effects are as expected,/ but for one: my pubic hairs fall out.' Although there is no chronology for her work, it appears from this second collection that her own forthcoming tragedy did not stop her expressing sympathy and sorrow for others. From her own childless condition, she can depict the agonised prayer of a young Spanish widow who, as the title says, is 'Crazy for another baby'. Then there is the pudgy three-year-old who launches himself off the Columbus monument, the veteran of the Civil War who returns alive, but horribly damaged psychologically, and the courage shown by 'The baker of Baghdad' who continues supplying his essential product from his basement during the Iraq war. In other poems we read movingly of the tensions in her childhood family and in her education. Less sensational but equally moving are the relationships the poet had at home with her dogs and cats and nature in her garden and the countryside. Most poignant of all are when she engages with the relics of orthodox Catholicism in poems such as 'The Infant of Prague', 'Stigmata', 'Plaint', 'Lady of Sorrows, and 'Sister Death'. But there is macabre knockabout comedy in 'If I should wake before I die', a pithy quatrain that ends "I'll make a spongy apple pie" and 'Philomena McGillicuddy becomes unstuck'

where the subject succumbs to the lure – or desperation – of private pleasure.

Most ambitious are the excursions into full-blown poetic biography, that is, biography in poetic form. 'Forbidden Fruit', published in her third collection *Long-distance Swimmer*, follows the life of Federico Garcia Lorca, whose thirty-eight eventful years are skilfully condensed into a series of resonant scenes in eighty three lines, leading to his death by Fascist militia in the heart of the countryside that inspired his poems. At even greater length, 'The loneliness of Catherine the Great' is one of the forty unpublished poems included in the present collection. This is a study in twenty one stanzas of varying length in the Russian monarch's own voice that captures the irony of her 'loneliness' while cataloguing the many lovers she had, most of whom merit pithiness or pathos in a thumbnail sketch as to looks, personal qualities and merit in bed. As a study in female desire, still a largely unexplored subject despite several popular sensationalist novels of recent decades, it is strikingly forthright, even if the great lady has most of these men chosen for her by other men and tested out (for one night only) by two of her entourage, the Ladies Bruce and Protasova. How All Russia was governed throughout her long reign is barely mentioned, but we do learn that outside the bedroom, she made generous gifts of land, jewellery and hard cash given to the fortunate lover. The more athletic, the greater the reward.

The previously unpublished work here shows how much promise there was in a poet who only began sending her work out in the decade before her decease. Although you would not gather it from the poems, the tragedy is overwhelming; but Molloy had not long to endure, dying in January of the following year, having just seen advance copies arrive of her first book, *Hare Soup* (2004). Ably curated by her widower, Andrew Carpenter, a further selection was made from her papers in *Gethsemane Day* (2006) and a final selection was published by Salmon Poetry in 2009 under the title *Long-Distance Swimmer*. All three volumes are published here in full, along with a selection of forty unpublished poems and four 'poems in progress'. These are included in the hope of encouraging scholars to 'delve deeper into the archive', as Professor Carpenter says in his 'Notes on the Edition'.

What is especially alluring about this archive are the comments on poetry that the editor has added to this edition. Although she came relatively late to poetry, having first begun to send her poetry out to magazines in the 1990s, she had obviously thought very deeply about poetry and especially so towards the end. The collection opens with a series of 'notes to self' under the title 'Credo' which was 'found in the notebook in which [she] wrote her last poems'. In a few tight phrases she reaffirms her faith in life; indeed, in God and the cosmos. It is terribly poignant – under the circumstances – to read the following selection:

> Art is the flame...Cut and burn
>     away to the truth... And keep two
>     feet on the ground.
> Let me connect to the universe
>     with my feet...

One is tempted to conclude that the poet's call is for an almost oxymoronic pedestrian transcendentalism here, but a proper conclusion would say that her vision of connectedness to the universe comes from being based in concrete imagery from reality and in reported sensations of that connectedness. This seems to me the core of what her work is about. Keeping two feet on the ground, grounding the work in reality and yet showing its transcendent qualities in many diverse and unexpected ways. She was a successful visual artist before she turned to poetry and this must surely have developed her eye for the telling image in poetry. This is nowhere better expressed than in the now published 'Alcossebre' sequence which revels in its sensuous impressions of the Catalonian sea and countryside and the feelings of exultation they elicit. But it is how she deals with crossing to a different country altogether that shows Dorothy Molloy's faith and inner strength.

## The Tower of Years

Anne Stevenson, *Completing the Circle* (Bloodaxe Books) £10.99
Reviewed by Sue Leigh

In her latest book, *Completing the Circle*, Anne Stevenson (now in her eighties) surveys her past from what she calls 'the viewpoint of a bewildered survivor... these poems cannot help facing up to the realities of time passing and beloved contemporaries dying'. This beautifully conveys a sense of the book as a whole.

The collection is a mixture not only of forms (sonnets, lyrics, meditations, narratives, lighter pieces) but also of themes and approaches. Its shifts of mood and subject matter (including science, music, philosophy, history), Stevenson suggests, might be considered part of the process of ageing.

The book opens and closes with a sonnet. The first, 'Anaesthesia', mourns the loss of friends 'so long depended on / To warm deep levels of my memory'. Yet this, she thinks, needs to be accepted with a kind of stoicism: 'There's nothing we can do but let it be'. Diminished, though, by these losses, she concludes: 'There's less and less of me that needs to die./ Nor do those vacant spaces terrify'.

There are elegies – for artists such as jazz singer Sandi Russell, poet Lee Harwood, pianist Bernard Roberts – and for a friend from high school days in Ann Arbor, Michigan. A blue-glazed bowl (another gift from a friend) 'holds my thoughts of you / choosing the bowl, and your thoughts / choosing it for me'. In this way a kind of 'afterlife becomes / as in your paintings, possible'. This is not to do with memory exactly or conversation; she describes these encounters thus: 'Like poetry / your visits are unpredictable, / meetings of minds / free of bodies and words on a common shore / of places and times'.

The title poem (which owes a debt to Rilke) remembers another friend and also a sister-in-law. Death, the poet realizes, has to be accepted as the complement of life: it 'completes the full circle / of a life's yearning'. (Kandinsky's *Several Circles* on the cover, consisting only of coloured circles on a black background, is pure abstraction.)

One might think that such subjects would make these poems sombre, but the poet's seriousness is frequently lightened by wit. There is no self-pity in the remembering, and often there is a sense of detachment around painful feelings. Among the elegies are lighter poems, such as a thank-you note to her dentist and a poem/Christmas card. The nine-line 'Candles' is a perfectly judged combination of spiritual concern – and irony. 'Choose to be a Rainbow' is a witty take on Richard Dawkins and ideas of immortality.

Stevenson has written and lectured on poetry with great authority for many years. 'How Poems Arrive', dedicated to Dana Gioia (and written in *terza rima*), expresses her belief that it is only in the process of being written that a poem reveals its meaning. 'But something like a pulse must integrate / The noise a poem makes with its invention. / Otherwise, write prose.' To write a poem is to hear it as it forms in the mind. In 'Now We Are 80', dedicated to friend and poet Fleur Adcock (at one time they were the only two women poets on the Oxford list), Stevenson offers this advice: ' a poet should, / For first and last things, trust to poetry. / Then, for a life style, choose simplicity.'

Birds fly occasionally throughout the pages of this book. Stevenson considers the song and behaviour of 'the bully thrush', and watches magpies and jackdaws from her back window, but I like best the robin that feeds from her trowel, and leaves her wondering why 'I feel so honoured'.

The last section of the book consists of two long autobiographical narratives. The first, 'Pronunciation', recalls friends and episodes in Stevenson's life when she was teaching in England in 1954–1955. The second, 'Mississippi', remembers a time in the 1960s when Stevenson lived there and races were segregated.

The book ends with the sonnet 'At 85'. The poet looks 'from the tower of years I call my life' and offers these possibly consolatory thoughts: 'Life will be mine as long as my mind is me. / While youth? Its wounds, anxieties and pain / Are best remembered, not endured again.'

## André Mangeot

André Mangeot, *Blood Rain*
(Seren) £9.99
Reviewed by Alastair Llewellyn-Smith

*Blood Rain* is André Mangeot's third collection of poetry, his first since 2005, his first from Seren. In that interval he has published two volumes of short stories, *A Little Javanese* (2008) and *True North* (2010). This new collection of fifty-three poems, divided into four sections, covers a wide ground, and is best summed up, perhaps, by a line from the very first poem, *Oxbow*:

> The breath
> of memory, and something else,
> across our shoulders.

There are sonnets in various guises, elegies for dead friends or relatives, love poems, and narrative poems. He has a sharp eye, and uses the sound and feel and taste of his words to capture his images. His rhythms change to match the physical exertion he's describing. *Heart*, an account of climbing with a companion in the Lake District, begins energetically: 'Impatient, our first afternoon/we boot straight up, waterproofs and rucksack//strike out through the mizzle', slows down as the climb gets tougher 'Skin chilling as the cloud-mists settle,/ weaves and licks around the map, the dotted track/we hold but cannot see ...' and collapses at the summit/climax:

'helpless, weeping on the mountain –//and you there in your rattling hood, brim-full of it.'

His use of places, the outdoors, is an effective route to memory. In the tender love poem, *Oxbow*, he writes, '... the river turned its back and took another path'. This recalls a precise image but also Thom Gunn's 'the river turns to see/Whether you follow still' (*In Praise of Cities*), and loses nothing by the comparison.

There's quiet courage, too, in this collection. Mangeot doesn't mind risking a reader's irritation by sometimes using esoteric titles. My initial frustration with *Uhtceare*, for example, was replaced by admiration when I realised that the poem itself was a delicate translation of the Old English word which names that anxiety we experience when we awake just before dawn and cannot get back to sleep! Nor does he shy away from drawing our attention to better-known poets. *Hawk* made me think of Ted Hughes' *Hawk Roosting* until the sub-title, *St Hywyn's Church, Aberdaron*, set the poem itself squarely in R.S. Thomas' country where ' ... storm-gusts, a silent/but beady kestrel, buffet and circle your parish'. Or is it a sense of kinship, poetic fraternity, that Mangeot wants to claim and share?

His elegies are understated, recalling dead relatives or friends with dry-eyed but poignant affection:

> Back home, at a loss
> we sift on in silence
> pull one more shoebox
> from under your bed
>
> and holding this card
> l can hear you again,
> seem right at your side
> as l never was then –
>
> (*History*)

His emphasis on relationships, on human interaction, doesn't mean he ignores (in *Jerusalem* or *The Odds*) the destructive aspects of our natures, what Christianity terms sin, a risible concept to many today; but Mangeot alludes frequently and easily to Christianity – another form of courage – as in *A Rosary*: "Weep/ with us, Lord, for how it is now, for how it will end. Amen."

He's good, too, at pared-down narrative poems which depict a whole human life in just a few lines, like Toulouse Lautrec's economical but all-encompassing pen-and-ink sketches.

> Now, silenced by the stroke, you signal me / to tap out your tablets. Here they sit, pillboxes / next to your chair: little white drums, / each one a depth charge, primed for attack.
> (*Depth Charge*)

Launching a new book in a time of pestilence is not ideal; there are no opportunities for public readings, for taking the new work on tour. This is particularly cruel for a long time performer (and member of The Joy of Six) and his new collection *Blood Rain*, since it is very much a book for these times, but also for the better time which we all hope lies ahead. I have returned to it again and again.

## On Michael Anania

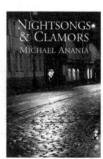

Michael Anania, *Continuous Showings* (MadHat Press) £18.90
Michael Anania, *Nightsongs & Clamors* (MadHat Press) £18.90
Reviewed by Ian Pople

Michael Anania is nothing if not prolific. These two substantial books are only a year apart and Anania's eighteenth and nineteenth. And, although we might admire fluency, profusion tends to be regarded with suspicion. Perhaps it's the simple pleasure of holding a poet's life work in a small volume, in which it's possible to observe a coherence, than carrying around a hefty double volume of seeming sprawl. As gorgeous as much of A.R.Ammons' voluminous work is, there's a comfort in picking up Elizabeth

Bishop's meticulously honed *Collected*. Michael Anania is cited in the tradition of modernism that starts with Pound, moves through Olson, Creeley and Lorine Neidecker, and perhaps rests today in a poet like Michael Teller. Sometimes this tradition is known as Objectivism; defined by Fiona McMahon as 'affirming the need for a greater attentiveness to the language of poetry and an acute awareness of the perceptual realities that shape one's immediate circumstances'.

*Continuous Showings* begins with a preface from Reginald Gibbons, which, after suggesting that Anania is 'synaesthetic', contains the following: '[Anania] makes melody and sentence and sight his primary colours, and he names them in his poems while simultaneously using them to mark the sharp edge – the precise and delicate edge – of his seeing and sentencing.' This might be one kind of paraphrase of McMahon's definition of Objectivism. Although there is, perhaps, some circularity in suggesting that sentence and sight mark the edges of seeing and sentencing. To some extent, as well, Gibbons' comment rather reduces the point that there are a number of Michael Ananias on display in these two volumes. In the sequence 'Omaha Appendices', Anania provides us with quietly drawn family portraits. There are four of these 'Appendices' in *Continuous Showings* and two more in *Nightsongs and Clamors.* These portraits of his family reach back to his great grandparents; portraits of their Italian diaspora 'in a corner of Omaha still called Florence Station.' Here there is hospitality of epic proportions, and they speak 'Calabrese / and English, sentences beginning in one / language and ending in the other. / At six or seven I understood everything / they said and almost nothing they meant.' These are unadorned but carefully and evocatively written, and Anania is good at summoning up family and domesticity without sentimentality.

Anania places these families, and particularly the men, within the mythology of the American twentieth century; 'my Uncle Frank, *Life* magazine's "Omaha / guy on Omaha Beach," stiff with shrapnel,/ my

Uncle Tony, home from the Philippines, / stabbed, he said, forty times in the heart, / just out of the frame on Iwo Jima'. Anania's ironizing of the mythology of war, is deepened by pulling the family members into its frame. The sweep through twentieth century history extends to a sweep through American culture. Anania writes well about jazz, and like many jazz afficionados, picks out figures who appeal to him and who might not be that widely known. In 'Four for Orbert Davis', a tribute to the trumpeter and founder of the 'third stream' playing Chicago Jazz Philharmonic, Anania begins, 'measured, time after time, what you insisted / upon, quiet gaining its own presence; alas, / to speak at all is to presume; presumption / thus proposes speech, speech, in time, music;' We can have too much of this slightly vatic attention to how speech and music interact.  But Anania, like Pound and Bunting, is a poet who listens carefully to music and the way the techniques of music offer equivalences in poetry. Like Bunting, too, Anania is familiar with the early music of Dowland and Vicenzo Galilei, Galileo's father. Anania is also the kind of poet who uses both this kind of meditation and the accumulation of imagery to achieve the kind of 'awareness of perceptual realities' that McMahon suggests.

Another of Anania's 'strategies' is to number each verse, even where the verses are short, or where such divisions cut across syntactic and sense units. Such deliberate disruptions might simply feel tricksy or jarring if used too often but Anania is tends to use disruptions where they contribute to a view of a diverse or fragmenting vision. In such poems, there is an accumulation of imagery as if a prism were being turned. Elsewhere, as we have seen, Anania is capable of space and range, from the intimately physical to empathies with historical figures and their actions. In 'Undivided Acts' from *Continuous Showings,* Anania muses on Paris in 1922, when Einstein, Satie, Ernst, Eluard and Marie Curie were all in the city at the same time. As the title of the poem suggests and as Anania writes in the poem this is a moment where 'all that their shared durations shared'.

This ability to see both the fragmentation and the continuity adds up to a poetry of satisfying heft and vision.

## The World is Dark but the Wood is Full of Stars

Seán Hewitt, *Tongues of Fire* (Cape Poetry) £10
Reviewed by Sue Leigh

Seán Hewitt's *Tongues of Fire* is a beautiful book, thoughtful, tender. It is an assured debut collection. The poems live among trees, plants and creatures – a world encountered with reverence. There is darkness here, decay, but also love, light, a sense of the sacred. The opening poem, 'Leaf', with its repeated 'for', has the quality of a prayer of thankfulness: 'For even in the nighttime of life / it is worth living, just to hold it'. 'Ilex' also becomes a prayer (for a newborn child) as the poet, coming across a cluster of pale holly at the base of a tree, imagines it becoming a crown that 'the people approach one by one / to witness how a fragile thing is raised.'

There are a number of epiphanies, 'Evening poem' for example, in which a mother and son, unspeaking, share the 'stifled warmth' of the greenhouse. The luminous moment, its intensity, is held in the image of the dove in the garden 'like a paper lantern...bobbing / in the appleblossom'. In the poem 'In Prince's Park', the speaker feels as if he has sleepwalked there and woken as a woodpecker 'shakes hold of the quiet – / its echo / ricocheting, knocking / at each tree for the unsuspecting / bright splint of life'. In 'Clock', he leans on a cedar, senses the tree as stillness, 'a circle of quiet air'.

The central section of the book consists of translations, or reimaginings, from the Irish *Buile Suibhne*.

(Hewitt is a teaching fellow at Trinity College Dublin.) This story – of the mad exiled king who composes poetry as he wanders – has inspired many writers, including Eliot and Heaney. Suibhne travels the countryside mourning the loss of his home: 'It is hard / to be without the sound of children / or music or the voices of women, / and it is cold, cold for me now'. Eventually he is wounded, confesses and dies. His friend Moling mourns for him: 'Glen Bolcain seems lovely to me / because Suibhne loved it, / and its clear, high streams / and its crop of watercress.'

There is a sense of freshness, an immediacy, in these poems. We sense a mind working out how nature might inform a way of thinking, being, understanding. In 'Wild garlic', the 'spiked white flowers light the way', leading to the revelation, 'The world is dark / but the wood is full of stars.' Watching barn owls in Suffolk, the poet wonders what it might mean to see them hunting in daylight: 'there is something in the slow / spread of the wing, the moment / of inverted flight, the living thing / pulled from the earth and lifted.'

The physical body also reads the world. In 'St John's Wort' (a poem that comes full circle) the speaker is asked to leave his gathering of flowers at the door when visiting a sick friend. 'Bringing no gift, I took your head / in my empty hands like a world and held it.' And in 'Häcksjön' the poet plunges into the black glass of a lake and loves to make it echo with his body; he 'plumb[s] its deep core'.

In the moving title poem (positioned last in the book), the poet tries to make sense of his father's dying, mortality and the nature of God. He observes the orange horns of the rust fungus growing on juniper trees. They remind him not only of the Pentecostal flame but also of the vulnerability of the body, its susceptibility to disease. He asks 'over and over / for correlation – that when all is done, / and we are laid down in the earth, we might / listen, and hear love spoken back to us'.

## On Hirschfield

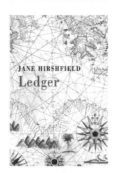

Jane Hirshfield, *Ledger* (Bloodaxe) £10.99
Reviewed by Jennifer Wong

Intelligent, complex and full of clarity, Jane Hirshfield's latest collection *Ledger* is a call to one's sense of justice and moral responsibility in the world we live in: a personal, ecological and social reckoning. One of the remarkable strengths of this book is to call into question our world-views, the way we measure or weigh our dilemmas.

Marked by its conciseness and silences, Hirshfield's poetry transports the reader from one place to another, while it opens up new vistas of understanding. Take, for example, what is asked of the reader in 'Things Seem Strong':

Things seem strong.
Houses, trees, trucks – a chair, even.
A table. A country.

You don't expect one to break.
No, it takes a hammer to break one,
a war, a saw, an earthquake.

Without much warning, the speaker shifts her contemplation from sturdy furniture to the state of a country. As soon as our imagination of what a strong country is is evoked, the speaker takes away the stable ground beneath our feet, and questions how much – or how little – it takes for one to cause irreparable damage.

In her interview with the *Paris Review*, Hirshfield says: 'From the periphery, you can see more of the whole. From the center, any view will be partial. A poem is not a frontal assault, it is the root tendrils of ivy making their way into the heart's walls' mortar.' A Zen Buddhist believer and an accomplished translator of Japanese poetry, Hirshfield's poetry is marked by its

pared down language and poignant clarity. Written for the 2017 March for Science in Washington, D.C., 'On the Fifth Day' is a poetic fable about those who find themselves trapped and silenced in the world of fake news and unscientific truths. In the last stanza, she shifts deftly into examining the workers in the city who have toiled for the whole week:

Bus drivers, shelf stockers,
code writers, machinists,
     accountants,
lab techs, cellists kept speaking.

They spoke, the fifth day,
of silence.

Through the power of metaphorical language, Hirshfield interrogates profound, complex social-political issues of our immediate world by blurring the boundary between the past and the present, between the personal experience and its universal meaning.

In 'Ledger', the title poem, the poet uses Tchaikovsky's Eugene Onegin as a starting point ('Tchaikovsky's *Eugene Onegin* is 3,592 measures. / A voice kept far from feeling is heard as measured'), as she reflects on the infinite possibilities to measure the same object or experience. There is acknowledgement of the pressures of the world: 'What's wanted in desperate times are desperate measures', but at the same time, the poem shifts from music, languages, metaphysics to laws of Nature to bring home the value of hope, and the need for acceptance as one continues to hope in a reality not of one's own choosing: 'Ask all you wish, no twenty-fifth hour will be given.'

At the core of Hirshfield's poetry, one experiences the poignancy and fluidity of the lyric voice. 'My Glasses' – a set of meditative poems with titles starting with 'My' depicts the poet's active engagement with the world and the relationship between seeing and unseeing: 'Glasses can be taken off. /The world instantly softens, blurs.' In the poem, Hirshfield cites the doomed fate of the eminent Chinese poet and scholar in the third century, Lu Chi, who was executed on a false charge of treason:

Each of the Yangtze dead
had a mother, a father, wife,
    children,
a well, some chickens.
No, the largesse of glasses is not
    seeing.

At the same time, Hirshfield draws the reader's attention towards the distortion of truth in the ancient past that still happens today, and how an unjust regime can cause damage to its people.

Marked by the poet's humanistic visions, crystallised language and clarity of thought, Hirshfield's *Ledger* captures the vision of a world where both harmony and discord co-exist, where people struggle with warring ideals, but persevere with their beliefs despite all odds. It is a world that is at once personal and universal, as Hirshfield fuses re-visions of history and hopes for the future.

## On Forché

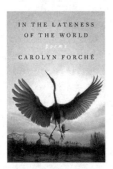

Carolyn Forché, *In the Lateness of the World* (Bloodaxe) £10.99
Reviewed by Jennifer Wong

Her latest collection after the widely-acclaimed *The Country Between Us* that establishes her work as a 'poet of witness', Carolyn Forché's *In the Lateness of the World* is an uncompromising, richly-textured and elegiac narrative on migration, crossings and social justice. Rich in intertextual references, the book prompts the reader to reflect on violence, the aftermath of history, and one's identity as a reader and writer, encouraging the reader to make connections between poetry and history.

The title of this collection draws from Robert Duncan's poem 'Poetry, a Natural Thing', prompting us to reflect on the role of art or poetry in times of political conflict, and the possibility to build a new world through the power of naming or the shaping of a voice: 'a call we heard and answer / in the lateness of the world / primordial bellowings / from which the youngest world might spring'. The epigraph of the book is taken from the French-Jewish-Egyptian poet Edmond Jabès, *The Book of Questions*, an aphoristic narrative that explores the painful condition of exile:

To those, finally, whose roads of ink
    and blood go through
words and men. And, most of all,
    to you. To us. To you.

Throughout the collection, the art of writing ('roads of ink') becomes a symbolic process of naming, seeking and healing, such as the contemplation of writing as '*older than glass but younger than music, older than clocks or porcelain but younger than rope*' in 'The Lost Suitcase'. In 'Elegy for an Unknown Poet', the first-person voice suggests that the poet is never dead, but continues to serve the living: 'I know that you are dead. Why do you ask and ask *what can be done?*'

Forché's poetic language is intuitive and politically engaged but at the same time appeals on a more personal level. Traversing different cultures and histories, many of the poems engage with specific historical incidents or are inspired by particular historical figures, calling into question the role of the poet as a witness to history as well as the necessity of translating history.

Quoting Humbert's last words from Nabokov's *Lolita* as the epigraph to the poem ('I am thinking of aurochs and angels, the secret of durable pigments...the refuge of art...'), 'The Refuge of Art' alludes to figures from art history, from the aurochs, or bison, of ancient cave paintings, in order to illustrate the retrospective value and lasting impact of art:

[...]It is not known why
he paints them, standing as he
    does in a slate blindness –
only that with time, he might
    decipher
a message regarding aurochs, bison
    and spirals, lozenges and stars.

As such, Forché contrasts what can be seen ('They also saw their own jeweled cities, their chess villages, quilts of crops, and snake of rivers') with what remain to be seen and can at best be documented through art ('only that with time, he might decipher / a message').

Dedicated to friend and fellow poet, Ilya Kaminsky, 'For Ilya at Tsarskeselo' evokes the grand imperial residence at Tsarskoe Selo in St Petersfield, where the young Pushkin, who – as painted by Illya Repin – once recited his poem before old Derzhavin in the Lyceum of Tsarskoe Selo. The poem considers some of the best-known artists and explorers in the world, suggesting the immortality and continuity of their discoveries:

On the day Michelangelo died in Rome, Galileo was born in Pisa.
Isaac Newton was born the year Galileo died. When they searched for the poet Kabir, they found nothing beneath his shroud but a sprig of jasmine.

Based on a poem from the famous Russian poet, Anna Ahkmatova, the ending reflects on the timelessness of writing: 'We are here now in one of the shrines of the silver poets. / You are one of the silver. The snow is a white peacock in a Russian poem.'

Divided into ten parts, 'The Ghost of Heaven' draws on Forché's latest memoir *What You Have Heard is True*, dedicated to her friendship with the intellectual Leonel Gómez, a friendship that has prompted her political awakening and activism. In the poem, the poet recalls her trip to El Salvador on the eve of the civil war:

Bring penicillin if you can, you
    said, surgical tape,
a whetstone, mosquito repellent
    but not the aerosol kind.
Especially bring a syringe for
    sucking phlegm,
a knife, wooden sticks, a clamp,
    and plastic bags.

Through Forché's incisive language and exact imagery, the poem captures apocalyptic moments of history or reimagined accounts of death from 'bones still sleeved and trousered' to the painful witnessing of '[w]alking through a firelit river / to a burning house', as the speaker acknowledges one's commitment to speak the truth: 'If they capture you, talk.'

Elegiac and profound, *In the Lateness of the World* demonstrates the poet's strength in blending narrative with testimony, and in balancing revelations and silences. With her assured voice and use of lyric, Forché forges a language of resistance, fleshes out an artist's commitment to his or her aesthetic judgment as well as reflection on moral responsibility. Shifting between a diverse range of places, languages and histories, Forché's works make connections between cultures and literary traditions, crystallising the role of the artist as an agent for collective memory and social change. Above all, through her dexterous use of form and poetic language, these haunting poems remind us of art as a unifying and healing force during and despite political change or crisis.

## Back to the Land

Jeremy Hooker, *Art of Seeing: Essays on Poetry, Landscape Painting and Photography* (Shearsman Books Limited) £16.95)
Reviewed by M. C. Caseley

Common Ground, the charity co-founded by the nature writer Roger Deakin, aims to promote 'local distinctiveness'. As a phrase, it roughly describes the commonality Jeremy Hooker seeks in his poetics. Seeking a sense of 'ground' through years spent living in Wales and the South of England, he gradually explored the sense of 'deep rhythms' he found 'embodied in the land itself, through the long interaction between human life and language and the physical groundwork of place'. It's no

surprise, therefore, that his poetry collections bear titles like 'Solent Shore' and 'Englishman's Road', nor that he frequently name-checks writers such as Edward Thomas and Richard Jefferies.

This handsome collection of essays, several of which first appeared in *PN Review*, is a companion volume to Shearsman's recent *Selected Poems*. Hooker's gradually developed readings of poets and painters, however, takes the reader through some unpredictable locations. The essays begin with Coleridge and the Welsh Modernist David Jones: the former's writings in *Lyrical Ballads* are described, in a revealing metaphor, as 'common bedrock', whereas the latter introduced Hooker to formal linguistic devices that evaded the vague pitfalls of self-expression. In a later essay, 'Gathering All In', the problems inherent in grasping Jones' entire corpus of painting and poetry are explored; Hooker, however, found the 'physicality' and 'materiality' of Jones' epic *The Anathemata* stimulated his ideas of depth through time.

Truffling beneath the surface of Heaney's essay 'Englands of the Mind', Hooker notes similarities between poets of place (Clemo, Bunting, Roy Fisher) but also teases out some of the tensions and contradictions in the ways poets such as Edward Thomas and Ivor Gurney had to negotiate patriotism and imperialism. An incomer in Wales, Hooker is alert to this, and the subsequent pieces exploring relatively obscure Welsh names show traditions being challenged by recent female writers. Whilst interesting, some of these seem a bit limited by being essentially brief book reviews, rather than sustained arguments.

Hooker is more involving when he negotiates class, registering his despair when encountering in Jones' work what he sees as Modernism's 'disdain for actual people', as opposed to 'a mythic 'People'', and instead tries to demonstrate how to celebrate the ordinary and the visionary together, in his poem 'Southampton Docks'. Extended readings of various English, Welsh and American poets seek this, shedding light on such writers as Charles Reznikoff, Peter Finch and Gwyneth Lewis. I particularly enjoyed

Hooker's encounter with the work of Roy Fisher, whom he characterises as 'a major modern poet in the Romantic tradition', a thought-provoking assessment.

Two lengthy essays attempt to weave together all these thoughts: the first concerns Mametz Wood, in the Somme area, and was written to accompany the recent photographs of Aled Rhys Hughes, showing the scarred but regenerated growth there. Here, in early July 1916, occurred a terrible First World War engagement, costing many lives from the 38th Welsh Division. Sassoon described it and David Jones uses it in *In Parenthesis,* describing 'the young men reaped like green barley, for the folly of it'. Hooker deftly explores the lingering Christian symbolism behind both poem and photographs, isolating the layers and fragments that provide a clear example of his poetics. He reaches a striking conclusion: 'what we know of the battle of Mametz Wood is poetry. This may be interpreted ... as vision.' In the final, largely autobiographical essay here, 'Putting the Poem in Place' (originally a Professorial Lecture), Hooker discusses some examples of his early work and continues to urge an exploratory openness on his students, something characteristic of all the essays included here.

## The Station Before

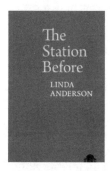

Linda Anderson, *The Station Before* (Pavilion Poetry) £9.99
Reviewed by Genevieve Stevens

Whether Linda Anderson's collection, *The Station Before* (Liverpool UP/ Pavilion) is looking to her past, present, dreams or the lives of others, its preoccupation is the same: to privilege seeing; to rapturously observe our lives so that we might uncover new meaning. The spirit of quest both binds these incongruent perspectives together and gives the collection pulse and intent. Anderson's voice, positioned at this frightening fault line of seeing/ unseeing, memory/imagination, past/ present arrives on the page quietly, with patience, sorrow and consideration. And how deftly she shifts – between precise, lucid poems about the past, to impressionistic poems that propel themselves behind the eyes of others, to abstract poems that gesture to the half-knowing of dreams and to mournful poems that despair of the present – a place of echoes, rubble, glimpses, wraiths, a place where nothing quite adds up: 'Always it's hard to know / what's real' the narrator quietly asserts in 'Fire'. These are not poems that manically dash about or shout for attention; their voice is poised and their shape largely contained in regular couplets, quatrains and sonnets. Anderson's language likewise does not push for idiom or explicit playfulness but quietly asserts itself through precision – a rapturous contemplation so focused on its subject it clears the page of ego.

Accompanying the poems across these great distances are birds – a veritable aviary of fulmars, ravens, kittiwakes, lapwings or just 'some creature [that] flutters through'. They are peculiar, elusive presences; entirely gathered into themselves, they arrive like a kind of shadow meaning, a migrating symbol too faint to fully grasp. 'Why Is a Raven Like a Writing Desk' describes the Japanese photographer, Masahisa Fukase, photographing ravens: 'Was it the stillness of photographs that fascinated him' the narrator asks, 'or a subject he strained to capture?' How to hold down seeing long enough to decipher meaning is beautifully explored in 'Intermezzo', a lyric and poised meditation on identity and the myth of arrival. 'This is a time of transition; it begins: 'the light is settling for less and less...// Our edges dissolve. / We put on our moth-faces.' The narrator's s voice is patient and vulnerable; between what is sensed and what is seen, she asks 'will the paths ever meet?'.

Given the dissolution of edges, it is unsurprising that self-identification in many of these poems is under threat. Anderson uses this frightening fenceless space to turn outwards and identify with others. Deftly she slips behind the moth-faces of writers, artists, philosophers – individuals who looked so hard at the world they were able to communicate new ways of seeing: Moore, Bishop, Saussure, Derrida, Nijinsky amongst others. In the first poem of the collection, the narrator transports herself behind photographer Felix Nadar. We are in Paris, 19th century, Nadar has launched his hot air balloon, with a 'laboratory / in the basket underneath' to capture the city like never before. The photos do not work, 'Nothing and yet again nothing. / A series all in black.' The balloon collapses, but still Nadar persists in looking, until eventually, something emerges:

But this time when I looked
I could see an image bit by bit
    appear

pale, masked by a hazy atmosphere,
stained by all the attempts there'd
been before.

Whereas the lives of others crackle with adventure, the narrator's own present reality is a site of intense, directionless longing. Even inklings, the gut-lunge, are 'blind'. Homesick for a time long-gone, the narrator must navigate the 'stones, shards, rubble, flakes of tile and plaster' scattered all about her. These are constrained poems; gesturing towards the speaker's desire for arrival, for knowing, for certainty, their own physical imperfection, where 'broken lines assail / and beckon', enacts the reality of falling short. Just look at this extract from the end of 'Disturbance':

There is a *slight* breeze, the *drawing*
    of breath, the *ghost* of
rain.
We sit at the kitchen table, our
    hands *almost* touching.' (my
italics)

Anderson ends the poem here but the breath is not exhaled just as the hands do not touch. Qualifiers 'slight' and 'almost' lessen significance. Even the ghostly rain cannot be the full-bodied fulfilment of its rain self.

Only the past, 'the station before', is a site of fulfilment. Depicted with clarity and colour, the narrator's childhood is relived in full sight. Lines harden around what is known; objects, people and places lie flat and unchanged: 'every morning when we woke / the smell of split wood flooded our senses' ('Bay'). In 'Haar', the narrator is dreaming of the lane leading to her childhood home, but 'the walls / on either side too high to see over.' In 'Cherries', the sweet fruit she once picked in her grandfather's orchard are no longer hers, but a faith in a bygone certainty persists:

Somewhere in the world they are
    still
growing cherries as they did in my
    childhood.

These two poems duet together, celebrating and mourning the small simple world of the narrator's childhood. Anderson dwells in the warm certainty of these fixed memories, and yet these moments are tinged with nostalgia, their contentment is quiet and unreal and often less affecting; like blue, a happy past always wants to recede whilst the present, red with unbelief and grasping, steps forward.

The handful of prose poems in the collection, for example '1953', in which the narrator remembers her grandmother, work less well. Despite some moving observations, the thinking can feel overcrowded, oversaturated: 'And there I must have been, a stranger, one of a cast of strangers passing through, blurring the edge of the frame, captured by change for a moment, moving into and out of visibility.' (Portrait) The lineated poem is perhaps a more suitable home for Anderson's plight of seeing / unseeing because it allows her to use the page's white space as breath and silence (there is huge weight and tension in her stanza breaks). It also enables Anderson to crack and let fall the lines on the right meaning or music, which she does so affectingly.

In 'Seven Descriptions of what Remains', Anderson lists the objects left by her father, and in a way the entire collection is a cenotaph to what remains: a woman in the act of writing, a daughter, a grand-daughter, her past bright and sure of itself, her present thinned out to 'almost colour'. *The Station Before* is a poetry of loss, yes, but it's also a collection that memorialises, with moving perception, the yearning we are left with, and the gratitude.

## Take It or Leave It

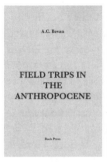

Dilys Rose, *Stone the Crows* (Mariscat Press) £6.00
A.C. Bevan, *Field Trips in the Anthropocene* (Rack Press) £5.00
Reviewed by Rory Waterman

The Scottish poet Dilys Rose is not well known, but she deserves a readership. If you're prepared to overlook the occasional flat line or sentiment, the often tidily and wittily observed poems in *Stone the Crows* are certainly enjoyable. To attune to them, one must embrace a certain cutesiness, most frequently exemplified in the anthropomorphising of animals, though Rose's warm, mildly anti-authority spirit is more akin to that of Wendy Cope than of any third-rate Georgian. In the title poem, a crow says:

> Darlin, I love how you tuck up your
> wingtips
> and snuggle up, but love your
> hoarse croak more,
> your final gripe before darkness
> undoes us.

In 'Murder of Crows' another compares its kind to 'gangsters, ministers', as though they are two sides of the same coin. 'Lamentation of Swans' pushes empathetically from the left margin:

> as the pen paddles
> in urgent circles
> frantic zig zags
> in any direction
> as long as it's away

and ends with 'the rat / which dined / at dawn // on her firstborn'.

If the Goth range of Sylvanian Families is not for you, perhaps you'll find something in 'Disworship of Scots' – in Scots lite – in which the animals are human:

> Prickly as thistles, they'll tak the
> hump
> as soon as look at ye. There's mair
> cheer
> in a month o sodden, Presbyterian
> Sundays.
> Nae need for tartan tams or ginger
> fright wigs
> tae gie us the heebie-jeebies – or
> the boak.

There are more human animals in 'Season Ticket for the Turkish', in which 'Old boy groans / slap off the dripping walls' of the steam room, as 'the old boys / deconstruct last night's game, brag of off-peak, / early-bird breaks on the Costa del Whatever', and try to sluice off intimations of mortality.

Occasionally, it all gets a bit much. The villanelle 'Sweetness', recklessly driven by its rhymes, serves little purpose other than as a warning that the ease with which one can write a bad villanelle can blind a poet to how difficult it is to write a good one. Nevertheless, there is an engaging, proudly unfashionable spirit in this work, perhaps best summed up by the pamphlet's closing line: 'It is just a poem. Take it or leave it. Either way, it couldn't care'.

Whether we 'take it or leave it', there is perhaps not very much we can do individually about the most inclusive crisis of our, and maybe any, age: the environmental catastrophe we are beginning to see unfold. How might a poet approach this existential threat? Many have tried – a whole world of what is now sometimes called 'eco-poetry' exists to confront it with puny little fists, which is all we have. The worst of this stuff is awful, carrying with it the whiff of the academic commission, complemented by unsubtle notes of moral superiority. I won't name names.

'Eco poetry' is not a term the late, great Peter Reading would've found very useful, one suspects. There is something of the spirit of the later collections of Reading in the wit and warning of A. C. Bevan's *Field Trips in*

*the Anthropocene*. This short pamphlet looks squarely into the abyss of our own making. The opening poem, 'This Week in History', reframes the Doomsday Clock as a Genesis parable, and takes us from 'the Precambrian dawn of Sunday morning' to:

> Saturday, we rounded Cape Horn/
> Good Hope,
> built telescopes, trains &
> Manhattan,
> invented the lightbulb, flight,
> penicillin,
> then spit the atom...
>
> & started again from the bottom.

If this was all the pamphlet had to say, and the only way it said it, there would be little to recommend. The seriousness of a predicament, or futility of a task, does not by itself a poem make, but the pamphlet's relentless parade of chilling reminders is frequently enlivened by cold, misanthropic wit, or acute observation or imagination. In 'Beached', the shrinking Dead Sea, for which 'irrigation, / drought & saline evaporation have / left a tidemark', is characterised by 'a fat man floating on / his back in a puddle'. In 'The Foragers', a 'tribe of hunter-gatherers / is picking through our wheelie bins' or 'in the wastes behind the Co-Op, / graingiver of stale crusts, / windfall of bruise-fruit'. Elsewhere, a fatberg is:

> A wayleave acre's
> length, the same tonnage & size
> as a dozen biofuel double-deckers
> rumbling over the grand design
>
> of the city's underground cloaca
> of Victorian plumbing, the lime
> pit where our habits & hazmats are
> flushed out of sight, out of mind.

And in the modern cities above, our 'Shards of Gherkins' are 'new cathedrals of glass ceilings'. This is poetry too economical and sprightly simply to be regarded as a panicked cry, though it is that too – and it perfectly suits the short format of a Rack Press pamphlet.

# Contributors

**Vahni Capildeo**'s themes are silence, crisis, and excess. **Anthony Rudolf**, a regular contributor to *PNR*, is a poet, translator and critic. He has published translations of Yves Bonnefoy, Claude Vigée and Edmond Jabès. Odd Volumes/ Fortnightly Review will publish his latest memoir, *Journey Round My Flat* at the end of the year. **Andrew Fitzsimons** was born in Ireland and lives in Tokyo. His books include *What the Sky Arranges* (2013); *A Fire in the Head* (2014); and *The Sunken Keep* (2017), a translation of Giuseppe Ungaretti's *Il Porto Sepolto*, all from Isobar Press. **John Clegg** works as a bookseller in London. **Alex Houen**'s first full collection of poems, *Ring Cycle*, was published in 2018. Along with Adam Piette he's co-editor of the online poetry journal *Blackbox Manifold*. **Alastair Llewellyn-Smith** is still working on his verse account of the 1974 Portuguese Carnation Revolution. **Martin Caseley** lives in Norfolk. He regularly contributes essays, articles and poems to *PN Review, Agenda* and *The Countryman*. He also reviews books for the International Times and Stride Magazine websites. **Rory Waterman** is the author of three collections from Carcanet: the PBS Recommendation *Tonight the Summer's Over* (2013), shortlisted for the Seamus Heaney Award; *Sarajevo Roses* (2017), shortlisted for the Ledbury Forte Prize; and *Sweet Nothings* (2020). **Ian Pople**'s pamphlet *Spillway* is published by Anstruther Press, Toronto. **Hilary Davies** has published four collections of poetry from Enitharmon: the latest, *Exile and the Kingdom*, in November 2016. She co-edited *Prophetic Witness and the Reimagining of the World, Poetry, Theology and Philosophy in Dialogue*, (Routledge, 2020). **Genevieve Stevens**' poetry, reviews and essays have appeared in journals in the US, Ireland and UK. She is currently doing a practice-based poetry Ph.D at Royal Holloway University, London. **Ned Denny**'s collection *Unearthly Toys* was awarded the 2019 Seamus Heaney Prize. *B (After Dante)*, a version of the Divine Comedy, is due out next year. **Jenny Eilidh Levack** is originally from Scotland and lives in Barcelona. **Andrew Mears** is a writer and musician based in Bristol, UK. **Mike Freeman** was an English lecturer in Manchester until he served his time on *PNR*'s and Carcanet's editorial team and is now a Pennine montagnard. **Andrew Hadfield** is Professor of English at the University of Sussex. *John Donne: In the Shadow of Religion* and *Literature and Class from the Peasants' Revolt to the French Revolution* will both be published next year. **Ian Brinton**'s translation of Baudelaire's 'Tableaux Parisiens' will appear next July from Two Rivers Press. **David Rosenberg**'s recent books include *A Literary Bible* (Counterpoint) and *A Life in a Poem (*Shearsman). **Sue Leigh**'s collection of poems, *Chosen Hill* was published by Two Rivers Press in 2018. **Victoria Kennefick**'s pamphlet, *White Whale* (Southword Editions, 2015), won the Saboteur Award for Best Poetry Pamphlet. A selection of her work will appear in Carcanet *New Poetries VIII* and her first collection is due out in 2021. **Beverley Bie Brahic**'s *White Sheets* (CBeditions) was a finalist for the Forward Prize. Her latest books are *The Hotel Eden* (Carcanet) and *Baudelaire: Invitation to the Voyage* (Seagull). **Ricardo Nirenberg** founded in 1998 and edits the literary journal *offcourse.org*. **Carola Luther** has two collections published by Carcanet Press – *Walking the Animals* (2004) and *Arguing with Malarchy* (2011). **Matthew Welton** is the editor of *The Threadbare Coat: Selected Poems* by Thomas A. Clark. He has published four books of his own poems with Carcanet, and a pamphlet with Thomas A. Clark's Moschatel Press.

# Colophon

**Editors**
Michael Schmidt
John McAuliffe

**Editorial Manager**
Andrew Latimer

**Editorial Assistant**
Charlotte Rowland

**Contributing Editors**
Vahni Capildeo
Sasha Dugdale
Will Harris

**Design**
Cover and Layout
by Emily Benton Book Design

**Editorial address**
The Editors at the address on the right. Manuscripts cannot be returned unless accompanied by a stamped addressed envelope or international reply coupon.

**Trade distributors**
NBN International

**Represented by**
Compass IPS Ltd

**Copyright**
© 2020 Poetry Nation Review
All rights reserved
ISBN 978-1-78410-835-9
ISSN 0144-7076

**Subscriptions—6 issues**
INDIVIDUAL–print and digital: £39.50; abroad £49
INSTITUTIONS–print only: £76; abroad £90
INSTITUTIONS–digital only: from Exact Editions (https://shop.exacteditions.com/gb/pn-review) to: PN Review, Alliance House, 30 Cross Street, Manchester, M2 7AQ, UK.

**Supported by**